Sync Mastery

Volume 2

© Copyright 2024 Music Of The Sea Inc

AF426374

"We love working with Eddie and Music Of The Sea - we always reach out to them first, they have the best music and are a pleasure to work with"

Maggie Phillips-
Music Supervisor. Fargo, Shogun, Snowfall, Hand Maids Tale

Contents

Foreword by Mathew Knowles

I've had the pleasure of working with Eddie Caldwell for over 20 years, and I can confidently say that his expertise in sync licensing is unparalleled. Eddie has a rare gift when it comes to identifying the perfect music for film, television, and commercials. His deep knowledge of the industry, combined with his impeccable ear for music, has earned him a well-deserved reputation as one of the best in the business.

Eddie's work with Music of the Sea has brought countless artists the recognition they deserve, and his contributions to the world of sync licensing have been invaluable. I trust his insight, his judgment, and his passion for music, and I know this book will be a tremendous resource for anyone looking to navigate the complex world of sync licensing.

Mathew Knowles
Founder, Music World Entertainment

1.1 Building Your Brand on Social Media

In today's game, if your social media hustle ain't tight, you're falling behind. Straight up—Instagram, TikTok, and YouTube are the major keys that can flip your whole movement from local to global. These platforms are where the right eyes are watching—music supervisors, producers, and, of course, the fans. But you can't just be another profile out here. Like Eddie Caldwell says, "You gotta pull up with purpose, show content that matches your vibe, and be consistent." It's all about owning your lane and staying on it, no breaks, no slacking.

How to Create a Strong Presence on Instagram, TikTok, and YouTube

Instagram: The Visual Showcase of Your Brand

Instagram is where your aesthetic meets your music. Think of it as your personal gallery where every post, story, and reel should contribute to a cohesive image of who you are as an artist. It's not just about posting pictures or snippets of your tracks—it's about creating a visual narrative that tells your story.

> *"Your brand is what people say about you when you're not in the room."*
>
> *– Jeff Bezos*

- **Leverage Instagram Stories and Highlights**: With Instagram Stories, you have the chance to engage with your followers in real-time, whether you're giving a sneak peek into your recording process or sharing clips from live performances. Highlights allow you to keep these stories accessible, organizing them into categories that speak to different aspects of your artistry—"Live Performances," "Studio Sessions," "Behind the Scenes," etc.

- **Reels for Music Discovery**: Reels are Instagram's answer to TikTok's short-form videos, and they've become a powerful tool for music discovery. Posting Reels that feature snippets of your music, paired with trending sounds or challenges, can introduce you to a wider audience. Be creative, but stay true to your brand—you want these videos to reflect your style and sound.

- **Collaborations and Tagging**: Don't underestimate the power of collaborations on Instagram. Whether it's teaming up with other musicians, influencers, or even visual artists, these collabs can help you reach a broader audience. Make sure to tag relevant parties and use hashtags strategically—this increases visibility and makes it easier for new followers and music supervisors to discover you.

TikTok: The Viral Playground

TikTok has revolutionized the way artists are discovered, offering an even playing field where anyone can go viral overnight. The key here is to keep your content authentic while taking advantage of the platform's trends.

- **Understand the Algorithm**: TikTok's algorithm thrives on engagement. Unlike other platforms, TikTok allows for a video to go viral even if you don't have a massive following. This means every post is a potential breakthrough. Keep your content relatable and engaging, whether you're hopping on trends, participating in challenges, or creating original, behind-the-scenes content that gives fans insight into your creative process.

- **Trends, but Make Them Yours**: Jumping on trends is a must for TikTok, but it's important to maintain your artistic identity. If there's a viral challenge or trending sound, find a way to make it your own. This keeps your content relevant while staying true to your sound and brand. If a music supervisor is scrolling through, you want them to see not just a musician, but a creative who knows how to adapt without losing authenticity.

- **Music Integration and Collaborations**: TikTok's strength lies in how easily it allows users to incorporate music into their posts. Share snippets of your tracks and encourage your followers to use your music in their own videos. This can snowball into organic exposure. Collaborating with TikTok influencers who vibe with your style can help get your music in front of thousands, if not millions, of users who may not have encountered you otherwise.

YouTube: The Hub for Long-Form Content and Monetization

YouTube is where you can dive deep. Whether it's through full-length music videos, live performances, or vlogs, this platform gives you the space to show all aspects of your artistry in greater detail.

- **Consistency Is Key**: On YouTube, success often hinges on consistency. Post regularly, whether it's a new music video, a live performance, or a vlog detailing your life as an artist. Keep your content fresh but always true to your brand. Consistent posting not only keeps your subscribers engaged but also signals to the algorithm that your channel is active, boosting your visibility.

- **Engage with Your Audience**: Use the comments section as a way to connect directly with your fans. Respond to comments, host Q&A sessions, or ask for feedback on new tracks or upcoming projects. Engagement makes your fans feel connected to your journey, and the more loyal your fanbase, the more likely they are to share your content with others.

- **Monetizing Your Content**: One of YouTube's unique benefits is its monetization capabilities. As your channel grows, you can start to earn revenue from ads, affiliate marketing, and sponsorships. This additional income stream can support your music career while also giving you the means to produce higher-quality content over time.

The Importance of Consistency and Brand Alignment

Your social media profiles are not just about promoting your music—they are an extension of your brand. Consistency in both content and brand alignment is essential for long-term success. Here's why:

- **Consistency Builds Trust**: When your audience knows they can expect regular, quality content from you, it builds trust. Whether it's daily TikTok posts, weekly YouTube videos, or regular Instagram updates, a consistent schedule keeps your followers engaged and shows industry professionals that you are serious about your craft. Music supervisors, agents, and managers want to work with artists who are reliable and dedicated to their brand.

- **Brand Alignment Creates a Clear Identity**: Your brand is the unique identity you present to the world. Every post, story, or video should reinforce that identity. Whether you're edgy, soulful, upbeat, or experimental, your social media content should reflect that consistently across all platforms. When your brand is clear, it makes it easier for music supervisors and potential collaborators to understand where you fit in the industry and envision how your sound could work in their projects.

- **Cross-Platform Integration**: While each platform has its unique strengths, maintaining consistency across all of them is critical. Use similar aesthetics, tone, and messaging on Instagram, TikTok, and YouTube. This ensures that when a potential fan or music supervisor comes across your content on one platform, they'll recognize you on others, building a cohesive and recognizable brand.

Final Thoughts: Mastering Your Online Presence

Building your brand on social media is an ongoing process that requires creativity, consistency, and authenticity. It's not enough to just post content; you need to make sure every post aligns with the image you want to project and the audience you want to attract. Keep your profiles polished, stay active, and engage with your followers regularly. The more you show up online, the more impossible it becomes for people in the music industry to scroll past you.

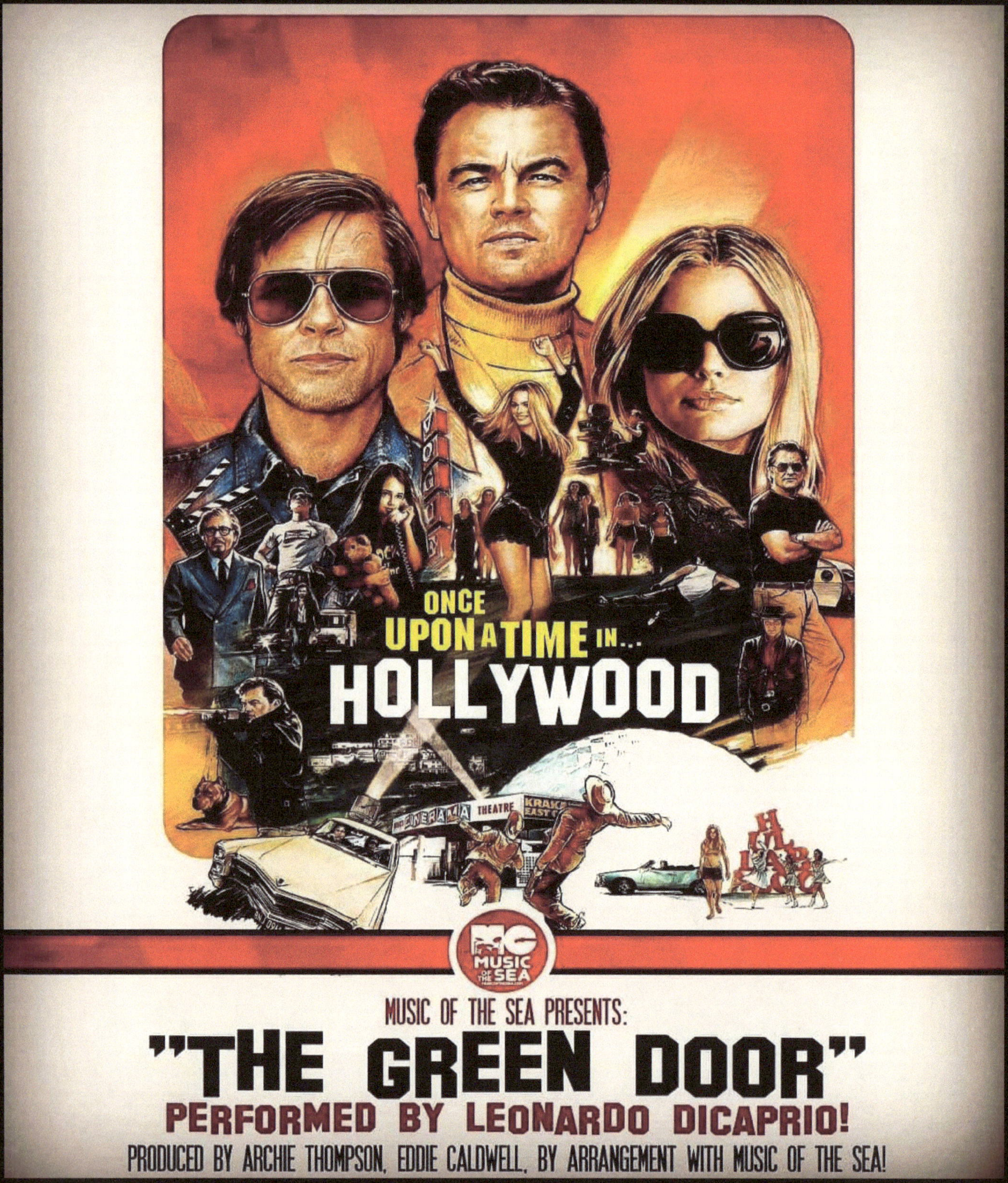

SONGS IN THIS FILM IS AN EXAMPLE OF MUSIC LICENSED BY EDDIE CALDWELL AND MUSIC OF THE SEA

1.2 Curating Your Content for Maximum Impact

In the wild world of social media, standing out is a must if you're trying to make waves. Your posts need to stop the scroll and grab attention within seconds. Platforms like Instagram, TikTok, or YouTube are where the game is won or lost, and the way you present your content is the difference between getting overlooked or catching the eyes of fans, potential collabs, or even key players like music supervisors. Eddie Caldwell's approach to this game? Keep it strategic, show off your creativity, and always stay authentic with how you represent yourself out here.

Tips for Creating Engaging, Scroll-Stopping Content

Know Your Audience and Speak to Them

The first step in creating impactful content is understanding your audience. What are they looking for? What resonates with them emotionally? When you know who your followers are and what they care about, you can create content that speaks directly to them. For musicians, this means balancing posts that highlight your music with content that shows who you are as a person. Fans often connect with artists whose personalities they can relate to, so sharing behind-the-scenes moments, personal reflections, or your journey in the industry can be just as important as posting music-related content.

- **Visual Appeal Matters**: Instagram and TikTok are visual platforms, and YouTube is a space for dynamic video content. Every image, thumbnail, and video should be high-quality and reflect your brand's aesthetic. Use colors, filters, and lighting that fit your style. For example, if your music is chill and mellow, you might opt for softer

tones and more intimate settings. If your sound is energetic and bold, your visuals should reflect that with vibrant colors, quick cuts, and dynamic action.

- **Tell a Story**: Whether it's through a series of Instagram posts, a TikTok challenge, or a YouTube vlog, your content should tell a cohesive story. Give your followers something to follow—a journey, a progression, or a behind-the-scenes look into your process. People love stories, and it's one of the most powerful ways to engage an audience. Think about how each post can contribute to the larger narrative of your career or personal brand.

- **Keep It Short and Snappy**: On platforms like TikTok and Instagram, where attention spans are short, your content should be concise and impactful. The first few seconds of a video are critical—hook your audience with an engaging introduction and a clear visual. On YouTube, while longer content is more acceptable, make sure your thumbnails and titles grab attention quickly. Give viewers a reason to click on your video over others.

Be Relatable and Authentic

Audiences crave authenticity. The days of perfectly polished, overly scripted posts are fading. While it's essential to maintain quality, showing your real self is equally important. Content that is too perfect can feel distant or unattainable, while more candid moments can build stronger connections with your audience.

- **Behind-the-Scenes and Raw Moments**: Don't be afraid to show the less glamorous side of your music career. Fans love to see the work behind the music—the late-night recording sessions, the rehearsals, and even the struggles you face as an artist. This vulnerability humanizes you and builds a deeper connection with your audience. On Instagram and TikTok, this can mean posting spontaneous stories or TikToks that show your creative process. On YouTube, you can take viewers on a full journey from writing a song to recording it in the studio.

- **Engage with Your Audience**: Respond to comments, engage with DMs, and ask for feedback. This not only keeps your followers active but also makes them feel valued. For example, ask your fans to suggest song ideas, or run polls to see what content they want to see next. Engaging directly with your audience can also give you invaluable insight into what resonates with them and what doesn't.

How to Use Hashtags, Trends, and Influencer Collaborations to Get Noticed

Master the Art of Hashtags

Hashtags are one of the simplest yet most effective ways to get your content in front of new eyes. Each platform handles hashtags slightly differently, but the principle remains the same—hashtags categorize your content and make it discoverable by people who may not yet follow you. To maximize their potential, you need to be both strategic and relevant with the ones you choose.

- **Research Trending Hashtags**: On Instagram and TikTok, there are always trending hashtags that can help increase the visibility of your posts. Keep an eye on these trends, but make sure they align with your content and audience. Jumping on a trending hashtag that has no connection to your brand can come off as inauthentic. Instead, find hashtags that are both popular and relevant to your music or message. For example, if there's a trend around #NewMusicFriday or #IndieArtist, use it to showcase your latest track.

- **Create a Custom Hashtag**: In addition to using trending and popular hashtags, consider creating your own. This can be especially effective when you're launching a new project, such as an album or tour. A custom hashtag like #YourNameTour2024 allows your

followers to join in the conversation, tag you, and make your content easier to find.

- **Don't Overdo It**: While hashtags are helpful, using too many can clutter your post and dilute its effectiveness. Stick to 5-10 highly relevant and targeted hashtags on Instagram, and around 3-5 on TikTok for each post.

Capitalize on Trends (But Stay Authentic)

Trends on TikTok and Instagram are fleeting but incredibly powerful. Being aware of viral challenges, sounds, or memes can give your content a huge visibility boost. However, it's important to adapt these trends in a way that still aligns with your brand.

- **Jump on Viral Sounds and Challenges**: If a sound or challenge is gaining traction, find a way to incorporate your music or style into it. TikTok's platform thrives on these viral moments, and by

participating, you increase your chances of reaching a wider audience. That said, not every trend will fit your brand, and that's okay. Choose wisely and only participate in trends that you can authentically adapt to your content.

- **Create Your Own Trend**: If you have a unique concept or sound, create your own challenge and encourage others to participate. On TikTok, this can be a great way to engage your audience and get your music in front of new people. You might create a dance challenge or encourage your followers to use a specific part of your song in their videos. By creating a movement around your music, you not only grow your reach but also build a community around your sound.

Collaborate with Influencers for Increased Reach

Collaborating with influencers can be a powerful way to amplify your brand and get your content in front of new audiences. Influencers often have established relationships with their followers, and a well-placed collaboration can introduce your music to thousands of potential fans.

- **Identify the Right Influencers**: Not all influencers are created equal. Find influencers who align with your brand and target audience. For example, if your music leans toward the indie or alternative scene, collaborating with influencers who have a similar vibe will feel authentic and create a stronger connection with their followers. Research influencers on Instagram, TikTok, and YouTube who have a significant following in your niche, and reach out with a collaboration proposal.

- **Collaborations that Make Sense**: Whether it's having an influencer use your music in their content or doing a joint post, the collaboration should feel natural. Forced or overly commercialized collaborations can feel inauthentic and turn off both your audience and the influencer's followers. Keep the content organic—perhaps an influencer uses your track as the soundtrack to their workout routine, or they feature your song in the background of a personal story they're sharing.

- **Mutual Benefit**: Collaborations should be mutually beneficial. When reaching out to influencers, offer something in return for their support, whether it's access to unreleased music, a shout-out on your platform, or even concert tickets. Building these relationships is key to growing your network and expanding your reach.

> **Do You Know?** *Do you know that using hashtags can increase engagement on your social media posts by up to 12.6%? Leveraging trending hashtags can boost your content's visibility and help you reach a wider audience. In 2023, 90% of top-performing posts on Instagram included at least one hashtag.*

Final Thoughts: Curate with Purpose

Curating your content is about more than just posting frequently—it's about posting with purpose. Every piece of content should serve your brand and engage your audience while staying authentic to who you are as an artist. Whether through engaging visuals, strategic hashtags, or influencer collaborations, focus on building a social media presence that makes people stop, listen, and remember you. The goal is to consistently create content that not only entertains but leaves a lasting impression on everyone who interacts with it.

1.3 Best Practices for Engaging with Followers

Tapping in with your followers is one of the realest moves to elevate your game and keep your fan base locked in. Social media ain't just about posting and bouncing—it's about creating a space where your people feel like they're part of something real. Eddie Caldwell knows the power of keeping your crew engaged, creating that community vibe where fans feel connected. The more they feel involved in your journey, the more they'll ride for you—sharing your music, showing up to your shows, and supporting your projects. Keeping it authentic and personal with your followers is how you build those lasting connections that matter.

Do You Know? *Do you know that 79% of consumers expect a response within 24 hours when they comment or message a brand on social media? Timely and meaningful engagement with your followers not only keeps them interested but also builds long-term loyalty. This kind of interaction also helps create a community around your music.*

Keeping Your Audience Active and Engaged

Consistency in Interaction

Just as consistent posting is crucial for brand visibility, consistent interaction is essential for maintaining follower engagement. It's not enough to simply put out great content—you need to actively involve your audience.

Every post should offer an opportunity for interaction,

whether it's through likes, comments, shares, or direct messages.

- **Respond to Comments**: One of the simplest yet most effective ways to engage your audience is by responding to comments. Acknowledge those who take the time to comment on your posts, whether it's with a quick "thank you" or a more personal response. This not only makes your followers feel appreciated but also encourages others to comment, knowing they might get a reply from you. On platforms like Instagram and TikTok, quick replies can turn casual followers into loyal fans.

- **Ask for Input**: One of the easiest ways to keep your audience engaged is by asking for their input. Create posts that invite feedback, opinions, or ideas from your followers. For example, you might ask for feedback on a new song you're working on or run a poll about which cover song they'd like to hear you perform next. This approach invites followers to feel like they are part of your creative process, which deepens their investment in your work.

- **Use Interactive Features**: Instagram Stories, TikTok live streams, and YouTube Q&A sessions are great tools for directly engaging with your audience. Features like polls, question boxes, and countdowns can create interactive experiences for your followers, encouraging them to participate actively in your content. Running weekly Q&A sessions where fans can ask about your music, creative process, or even your personal life can make them feel closer to you, keeping them engaged.

Create Shareable Moments

One of the best ways to engage your audience is by giving them content that they can't resist sharing with their own networks. When people share your posts, stories, or videos, they're effectively promoting you to a wider audience, helping you grow organically.

- **Highlight Fan Contributions**: If your fans are using your music in their own social media content, showcase it on your own profiles. Whether they've used your song in a TikTok dance challenge or shared a story about how your music inspired them, reposting or highlighting their content shows that you value your audience. This not only deepens engagement but also encourages more fans to create content with your music, boosting your visibility.

- **Create Viral-Worthy Content**: Curate moments that people want to share. This could be a particularly powerful lyric, a behind-the-scenes moment of raw emotion, or a humorous or lighthearted video. When you provide content that resonates deeply or is highly relatable, your followers will be more inclined to share it, helping you reach new audiences.

- **Encourage User-Generated Content**: Actively invite your followers to create content that features your music. For example, you could challenge your followers to create videos using a specific song, encouraging them to tag you so you can see and share their work. TikTok and Instagram are particularly well-suited for this type of engagement, and it not only promotes your music but also gives your followers a sense of involvement and recognition.

How to Use Feedback, Comments, and DMs to Build Stronger Connections

Value and Act on Feedback

Your followers are more than just fans—they are a source of invaluable feedback. Listening to their opinions, suggestions, and critiques can help you grow as an artist and refine your content.

- **Pay Attention to Comments**: Comments are a direct line of communication with your audience, and they often contain useful insights. If you consistently see fans praising a certain aspect of your music, take note—that's something to amplify in future releases.

Conversely, constructive criticism can help you identify areas where you might want to improve. Whether it's production quality, song choice, or content direction, take comments seriously and show your audience that you value their input by making adjustments based on their feedback.

- **Surveys and Polls**: Beyond casual comments, consider using polls or surveys to gather more structured feedback. For instance, you could run a poll asking which song your followers liked most from your recent album or use Instagram's question feature to let fans suggest new ideas for content. This not only gives you a clear idea of what your audience is interested in but also reinforces the idea that their opinions matter to you.

Leverage Direct Messages (DMs) for Personal Connections

Direct messages (DMs) offer an incredible opportunity to build deeper, more personal connections with your followers. While it's not feasible to respond to every DM, selectively engaging with messages can have a profound impact.

- **Acknowledge Your Fans**: Responding to DMs from fans can turn casual followers into loyal, lifelong supporters. If a follower takes the time to send you a message, whether it's about how much your music means to them or just a comment on your latest post, acknowledging them shows that you appreciate their support. Even a quick, "Thanks for the love!" can make a huge difference in how connected a fan feels to you.

- **Build Relationships with Industry Contacts**: DMs aren't just for fan engagement—they're also a useful tool for networking within the industry. If a producer, fellow artist, or music supervisor reaches out, take the time to engage professionally. The relationships you build in the DMs can lead to collaborations, sync deals, and new opportunities that might not have emerged through formal channels.

Personalization Makes an Impact

In an era of mass communication, personalized engagement stands out. When you take the time to acknowledge specific followers or respond to comments in a way that feels individual, you elevate the relationship from artist and fan to something more meaningful.

- **Shout-Outs**: A simple shout-out can go a long way in making your followers feel special. For example, if someone has been particularly supportive or if you notice a follower consistently engaging with your posts, give them a shout-out in your stories or on a live stream. This kind of personal recognition encourages deeper loyalty and motivates others to engage more frequently in the hopes of receiving similar acknowledgment.

- **Respond with Thoughtfulness**: Whenever possible, respond to comments and DMs with thoughtful, personalized replies. Instead of a generic "thank you," mention something specific about their comment, like "I'm glad you loved the guitar solo in my latest track!" This kind of attention to detail makes your followers feel seen and heard.

Final Thoughts: Meaningful Engagement Over Mass Interaction

Engaging with your audience isn't about responding to every comment or message—it's about creating meaningful, authentic interactions that make your followers feel connected to you and your journey. By consistently showing up in your comments, DMs, and through interactive content, you can build a community that not only supports you but actively contributes to your growth as an artist. Keep the dialogue open, listen to your fans, and make engagement a key part of your social media strategy. The more you invest in your audience, the more they will invest in you.

MARVEL STUDIOS
A JAMES GUNN FILM
GUARDIANS OF THE GALAXY
VOLUME 3
$845.6 MILLION
SONGS IN THIS FILM IS AN EXAMPLE OF MUSIC LICENSED BY
EDDIE CALDWELL AND MUSIC OF THE SEA

2.1 Preparing for a Live Showcase

Hitting the stage live is one of the biggest shots you got to flex your skills, vibe with new crowds, and leave a mark on industry heads. Whether you're rocking for fans, A&Rs, or music supervisors, every little detail counts—from the tracks you drop to the energy you bring. The mission? Not just to put on a dope show, but to craft an unforgettable moment that sticks with people. This section will show you how to lock in your setlist, connect on a real level with the crowd, and make sure your soundcheck is tight so your performance is nothing but fire.

How to Perfect Your Setlist and Connect Emotionally with the Audience

Crafting a Setlist with Intent

Your setlist is more than just a random selection of songs—it's a narrative that you want to guide your audience through. The songs you choose, the order in which you perform them, and the emotional journey you take your audience on can make the difference between a good performance and a memorable one.

- **Start with Energy, Then Build Momentum**: Open your set with a song that grabs attention right away. It should showcase your talent but also be energetic enough to pull the audience in from the start. Once you've captured their interest, strategically build momentum throughout your set. Alternate between high-energy tracks and more emotionally-driven songs to keep the audience engaged without overwhelming them. Too many fast-paced songs in a row can lead to

listener fatigue, while too many slow songs might lose the crowd's attention.

- **Create an Emotional Arc**: Consider the emotional journey you want to take your audience on. A well-constructed setlist has an emotional arc that mirrors the way great stories are told. Start strong, bring the audience to an emotional peak, and then ease into a soft, reflective moment before ending with a powerful closer. This helps keep your performance dynamic and ensures that your set leaves a lasting impression.

- **Know Your Audience**: When crafting your setlist, always keep in mind who you're performing for. Is it a showcase for industry professionals? If so, consider including songs that highlight your versatility and potential for sync licensing. If you're performing for fans, you might want to focus more on popular songs that they can sing along to. Tailoring your setlist to the audience's expectations ensures that your performance resonates with the people you want to impress the most.

Connecting with Your Audience on an Emotional Level

Great performers don't just play songs—they create an emotional connection with the audience. This connection is what transforms a set from a performance into an experience.

- **Engage Through Storytelling**: One of the best ways to connect emotionally with your audience is through storytelling. Introduce certain songs with a brief story about their meaning or inspiration. Sharing the personal significance behind a track allows the audience to feel closer to you and gives them context for your music. However, keep your storytelling concise—you don't want to disrupt the flow of the performance.

Be Present and Authentic: Audiences can sense when a performer is simply going through the motions. To connect on an emotional level, you need to be fully present and authentic in your performance. Don't be afraid to show vulnerability or to be spontaneous in the moment. Whether it's a subtle smile, a glance toward the audience, or an improvised riff, these genuine moments draw people in and create an atmosphere of shared experience.

Use Body Language to Amplify Emotion: Your physical presence on stage can amplify the emotional impact of your music. Move with purpose—don't just stand still throughout your set. Use your body to express the energy of each song, whether it's through subtle swaying during a ballad or dynamic movements during an upbeat track. Eye contact is another powerful tool. Scan the crowd and make brief moments of connection with individuals to create a more intimate experience, even in larger venues.

Invite Audience Participation: Another way to build an emotional connection is by involving the audience in your performance. Whether you encourage them to sing along to a chorus, clap in rhythm, or chant with you, these moments of participation create a shared experience. It also shifts the focus from you to the collective energy of the room, fostering a deeper emotional connection.

> *"An artist's job is to captivate… If we stumble into an audience that isn't ready to receive us, it's our job to win them over."*
>
> *– Quincy Jones*

Soundcheck Tips and Tricks for Live Performance Success

The Importance of a Thorough Soundcheck

The soundcheck is one of the most critical moments before your live showcase. It's your opportunity to ensure that everything sounds perfect, from your vocals to the instruments and backing tracks. A well-executed soundcheck sets the foundation for a smooth, professional performance.

- **Arrive Early and Be Prepared**: Arrive at the venue early, especially if it's a showcase where several artists will be performing. Soundcheck time can be limited, so be prepared to make the most of the time you're given. Bring any necessary equipment like in-ear monitors, backup microphones, or instrument cables. Have a clear idea of the levels you want for your vocals, instruments, and any backing tracks to avoid wasting time once you're on stage.

- **Check Individual Elements First**: Start the soundcheck by testing each element of your setup individually. Begin with the vocals, ensuring that your microphone levels are balanced and clear. Move

on to your instruments, checking that each one can be heard distinctly and doesn't overpower the vocals. Finally, test your backing tracks or any additional sound effects to make sure they're properly integrated into the overall mix.

- **Test from the Audience's Perspective**: Once you've balanced everything on stage, step off the stage or ask someone to stand in the audience area to hear how it sounds from their perspective. The mix may sound different from what you hear on stage, so it's crucial to adjust the levels accordingly. Make sure your vocals are crisp and that the instrumentation is clear without overwhelming your voice.

- **Be Mindful of Acoustics**: Every venue is different, and the acoustics of the room will affect how your performance sounds. Take a moment during soundcheck to listen carefully to how sound travels in the space. If you're performing in a smaller, intimate venue, your sound levels might need to be adjusted to prevent overpowering the room. Larger venues may require more volume to fill the space, so ensure that your levels are set appropriately.

Troubleshoot Common Issues

Even with the best preparation, issues can arise during soundcheck. Here's how to troubleshoot some common problems:

- **Feedback**: If you encounter feedback during soundcheck, adjust the microphone levels and reposition the speakers to avoid sound loops. Feedback usually occurs when microphones are too close to monitors, so repositioning can often resolve the issue.

- **Unbalanced Mix**: If your vocals or instruments are getting lost in the mix, adjust the levels to ensure balance. Often, bass-heavy instruments like drums or electric guitars can overpower the mix, so lowering their levels can help bring clarity to your performance.

- **Technical Failures**: Always bring backups for essential equipment like microphones, guitar strings, and cables. If a technical failure

happens during soundcheck, having spares on hand will prevent last-minute panic. It's also smart to have a plan for dealing with equipment failures mid-performance, such as switching to an acoustic setup if your amp dies.

Rehearse Transitions Between Songs

The flow of your performance is just as important as the songs themselves. Use soundcheck as an opportunity to rehearse transitions between songs. This could involve making sure your guitar is tuned for the next song or testing the timing of backing tracks. Smooth transitions keep the energy of your set intact and prevent any awkward pauses.

Final Thoughts: Preparing for a Stellar Showcase

Preparation is the key to making sure your live showcase leaves a lasting impression. By carefully curating your setlist to create an emotional journey, engaging with your audience through authenticity and storytelling, and executing a flawless soundcheck, you set yourself up for success. Remember, the goal of a showcase isn't just to perform—it's to connect, to move, and to leave an indelible mark on everyone who experiences your music. With the right preparation, every showcase can become a stepping stone to greater opportunities.

2.2 Commanding the Stage

Owning the stage is everything for any artist, no matter if you're shutting down a packed venue or keeping it laid-back with a smaller crowd. It's more than just dropping your lyrics or playing your set—it's about how you move, connect with the audience, and make sure all eyes are glued to you from the moment you step up. Eddie Caldwell always brings that energy, knowing a performance isn't just about the music, but about creating a moment that sticks. We'll dive into how to deliver that next-level stage presence, bring the heat, and vibe with the crowd to turn a regular set into something unforgettable.

Techniques for Making a Lasting Impression Through Energy and Stage Presence

Project Confidence from the Start

Confidence is the foundation of commanding the stage. Even if you're nervous, projecting confidence is essential to capturing and maintaining the audience's attention. This starts before you even play your first note.

- **Own the Moment**: The second you walk onto the stage, act as though you belong there. Your body language should exude confidence—stand tall, shoulders back, and walk with purpose. The audience will pick up on your energy, so if you're calm and confident, they'll be more likely to focus on you and your performance.

- **Make a Strong Entrance**: How you start your performance can set the tone for the entire show. Whether it's with a powerful opening riff, a dramatic pause, or an engaging greeting to the crowd, make sure your entrance grabs attention. Let the audience know from the first moment that they're in for something special.

- **Use the Entire Stage**: Don't confine yourself to one spot on the stage unless it's for a specific moment in the performance. Move around and use the space to your advantage. Engaging different areas of the stage helps you connect with more of the audience and makes your performance feel dynamic and full of energy. Whether it's walking to the edge of the stage during a guitar solo or stepping back during a quiet ballad, your movement should match the mood of the song.

Channel Your Energy to Fit the Mood of the Music

Not every song in your set will have the same energy level, and your stage presence should reflect that. Tailor your performance style to match the emotional tone of each track.

- **High-Energy Songs**: For upbeat, fast-paced songs, your energy on stage should match the intensity of the music. Use bold, dynamic movements—jump, dance, and move with the rhythm to amplify the excitement. These are the moments to let loose and show off your personality. Get the crowd involved by clapping along, dancing, or singing the chorus.

- **Slower, Emotional Songs**: When performing more emotional or reflective tracks, your stage presence should be more restrained but no less powerful.

Do You Know? *Do you know that the energy and stage presence you bring can increase crowd engagement by 40%? Artists who actively involve their audience during live performances leave a more lasting impression and are more likely to have their shows talked about, leading to potential booking opportunities and industry interest.*

- Use subtle movements, like swaying or a slow walk across the stage, to create an intimate atmosphere. Let the emotion of the song flow through your body language—lean into the microphone, close your eyes during key moments, and make sure your facial expressions convey the feeling behind the lyrics.

Master the Art of Eye Contact

Eye contact is one of the most effective tools for establishing a connection with your audience. It makes the performance feel personal and invites the crowd into your world.

- **Scan the Crowd**: Don't just stare off into the distance—make an effort to look at different sections of the audience throughout your performance. This helps create the feeling that you're performing for each person individually, even in a larger crowd. If the venue is smaller, try to make eye contact with specific individuals for a few moments before moving on. This personal touch can make your performance feel more intimate and engaging.

- **Use Eye Contact for Emphasis**: During key moments of your performance, lock eyes with someone in the audience to create a deeper connection. Whether it's during a particularly emotional lyric or a powerful instrumental solo, eye contact can amplify the impact of the moment and make it more memorable for the audience.

Body Language Speaks Louder Than Words

Your body language is just as important as your voice or instrument. It communicates your energy, emotion, and level of engagement with the audience.

- **Express Emotion Through Movement**: Use your body to express the mood of each song. For an energetic anthem, move with enthusiasm and confidence, using big gestures like fist pumps or wide arm movements. For more emotional songs, use smaller, more

deliberate movements that match the intensity of the lyrics. The key is to make your body movements feel natural and aligned with the song's message.

- **Use Gestures to Connect**: Gestures can be a powerful way to connect with the audience. Pointing out to the crowd during a lyric, raising your arms to get the audience involved, or reaching out as if you're inviting them into the experience creates a more interactive dynamic. These gestures make the performance feel less one-sided and help turn the crowd into active participants rather than passive observers.

How to Engage with the Crowd and Create a Memorable Experience

Acknowledge the Audience

A key aspect of commanding the stage is interacting with your audience. The more engaged they feel, the more memorable your performance will be.

- **Speak Between Songs**: Don't just play song after song without any breaks for conversation. Take the time between tracks to speak to the audience—introduce the next song, share a brief story, or thank the crowd for their energy. These moments of interaction make the performance feel more personal and create a connection beyond the music. It also gives the audience a chance to catch their breath and stay engaged with the flow of the show.

- **Compliment the Crowd**: Let the audience know how much you appreciate them. Whether it's commenting on their energy, saying how great the venue is, or shouting out specific people you see in the crowd, compliments make the audience feel good and build a positive rapport. Just make sure it feels genuine and not forced—audiences can tell when a performer is phoning it in.

Involve the Audience in the Performance

The more involved the audience feels, the more likely they are to remember the experience. Find ways to actively involve them in the performance.

- **Encourage Sing-Alongs**: Get the crowd singing with you during choruses or key moments in your songs. This creates a shared experience and helps the audience feel like they're a part of the show rather than just watching it. You can also invite them to sing parts of the song, especially if it's a well-known track—letting the audience take over the chorus for a moment can create a powerful, memorable connection.

- **Create Call-and-Response Moments**: Call-and-response techniques are a great way to engage the crowd. Whether it's repeating a simple phrase or clapping to a beat, this type of interaction keeps the energy high and the audience engaged. It also breaks down the barrier between the performer and the audience, making the performance feel more like a communal experience.

Tailor Your Performance to the Audience's Energy

Every crowd is different, and part of commanding the stage is being able to read the energy in the room and adjust your performance accordingly.

- **Adapt to the Vibe of the Crowd**: If the crowd is particularly energetic, lean into that energy by encouraging more movement, sing-alongs, or even improvising parts of your set to match their enthusiasm. On the other hand, if the crowd seems more reserved, focus on creating an intimate atmosphere. You might slow things down, engage with individual audience members more, or tell more stories between songs to bring them into the experience.

- **Be Spontaneous**: Don't be afraid to go off-script if the moment calls for it. Whether it's taking a request from the audience, extending a

song if the crowd is really into it, or changing the setlist on the fly, these spontaneous moments can create magic and make the performance feel unique. Audiences love when something special happens that they weren't expecting—it makes the show feel like a one-of-a-kind experience.

Final Thoughts: Making Every Performance Memorable

Commanding the stage is about more than just delivering a flawless performance—it's about creating an experience that resonates with the audience. By projecting confidence, using your body language effectively, and engaging with the crowd on a personal level, you can make your performance unforgettable. Each show is an opportunity to connect with your audience, build your fanbase, and leave a lasting impression that goes beyond the music. When you combine strong stage presence with genuine audience engagement, you elevate your performance into something truly memorable.

2.3 Case Studies: Artists Who Nailed Their Showcases

Showcases can be the springboard that takes an artist's career to the next level, giving you the chance to wow industry heads, lock in deals, and grow your fanbase. For some artists, that one fire showcase performance was the game-changer that got them noticed by the right people in the biz. Check out these real-life stories of artists who took the stage and used it as a launchpad to bigger moves and major stages.

Billie Eilish: The Breakthrough at SXSW

Billie Eilish is one of the most prominent examples of an artist who used a showcase to gain massive industry attention. In 2017, at the age of 15, Billie Eilish performed at South by Southwest (SXSW) in Austin, Texas—a festival known for giving emerging artists a platform to perform in front of industry professionals and music lovers alike. Eilish's showcase was highly anticipated following the release of her viral single "Ocean Eyes."

- **How She Nailed It**: Eilish's unique style, haunting vocals, and intimate connection with the audience helped her stand out in a sea of other performers. Despite her young age, she commanded the stage with a calm confidence, creating an unforgettable atmosphere. Her minimalist approach, paired with emotionally charged songs, resonated deeply with the audience.

- **Career Impact**: This performance at SXSW caught the attention of music executives and helped solidify her as an artist to watch. Following this showcase, Eilish's career took off, leading to major label backing, extensive touring, and her eventual rise to become one of the biggest names in pop music globally.

Chance the Rapper: Building Buzz at Lollapalooza

In 2013, Chance the Rapper was still an independent artist when he performed a highly praised showcase at Lollapalooza in his hometown of Chicago. While not technically a traditional "showcase," Chance's Lollapalooza set was his opportunity to shine on a big stage in front of key industry players. This performance was pivotal for him as it coincided with the buzz around his critically acclaimed mixtape *Acid Rap*.

- **How He Nailed It**: Chance the Rapper used his hometown advantage and charisma to engage the crowd, delivering a high-energy, engaging performance that highlighted both his musicality and his unique approach to hip-hop. He built an emotional connection with the audience by reflecting on his journey as an independent artist, making the performance feel personal and authentic.

- **Career Impact**: The performance was a turning point in Chance's career. It generated significant media coverage and industry buzz, leading to major collaborations with artists like Kanye West. Chance continued to grow his career without signing to a major label, making his performance at Lollapalooza a defining moment in his path toward Grammy wins and commercial success.

Lizzo: Going from Local Talent to Global Star at SXSW

Before she became the powerhouse performer we know today, Lizzo was a rising artist trying to break into the mainstream. In 2014, Lizzo performed at SXSW, which was an important moment in her journey. At the time, she was gaining local attention in the Minneapolis music scene, but SXSW provided a larger platform for her to showcase her talent in front of industry insiders.

- **How She Nailed It**: Lizzo's bold, energetic stage presence immediately captivated the SXSW crowd. She was unapologetically herself, mixing rap, soul, and pop in her performances, all while

exuding confidence and body positivity. Lizzo's authenticity and infectious energy made her stand out in a festival lineup packed with emerging artists.

- **Career Impact**: While Lizzo didn't achieve instant mainstream success after SXSW, the showcase performance helped her build industry relationships and secure media attention. This early buzz eventually led to collaborations and record deals that would later launch her to superstardom, culminating in her breakthrough with hits like "Truth Hurts" and "Juice."

Ed Sheeran: From Open Mic Nights to Industry Buzz at The Bedford

Before Ed Sheeran became a global sensation, he was known for relentlessly performing at open mic nights and small venues. His performance at The Bedford in London—a venue known for showcasing up-and-coming talent—became a key moment in his early career. In 2010, Sheeran performed at a showcase that included several music executives and influential figures in the British music scene.

- **How He Nailed It**: Sheeran's performance at The Bedford was simple, with just him, his guitar, and a loop pedal. His ability to engage the crowd with his soulful voice, relatable lyrics, and raw authenticity made him stand out. The intimate setting of The Bedford allowed him to connect emotionally with the audience, demonstrating the depth of his talent and songwriting ability.

- **Career Impact**: Following this performance, Sheeran gained the attention of industry professionals, which led to a record deal with Atlantic Records and the release of his debut album, +, in 2011. The success of that album, driven by hit singles like "The A Team," catapulted Sheeran into international stardom.

Dua Lipa: From YouTube Covers to Warner Music

Dua Lipa's rise to fame can be traced back to her early showcases and performances, which helped her transition from an internet sensation to a pop superstar. In 2015, Dua Lipa performed at a series of industry showcases that were pivotal in securing her record deal with Warner Music Group.

- **How She Nailed It**: Lipa's showcase performances were marked by her powerful voice, charisma, and ability to command the stage. Despite being relatively new to live performances at that time, she exuded confidence and performed with the poise of a seasoned artist. Her vocal ability, combined with her edgy style and pop appeal, made her a standout in front of record label executives.

- **Career Impact**: These early showcases helped Lipa secure a contract with Warner Music Group, which led to the release of her debut album in 2017. The album's success, particularly with hits like "New Rules," solidified her place in the pop industry and set her on the path to becoming an international superstar.

> *"Success is where preparation and opportunity meet."*
>
> *– Bobby Unser*

SONGS IN THIS TV SHOW IS AN EXAMPLE OF MUSIC LICENSED BY EDDIE CALDWELL AND MUSIC OF THE SEA

"It's been great working with Eddie over the years. Always on point with music he's sent my way!"

Justin Kamps -

3.1 Mastering the LA Music Scene

LA is the heartbeat of the entertainment world, and the music scene here isn't just competitive—it's full of opportunities if you know how to navigate it. Making a name in this city means understanding the culture and knowing how to move. From exclusive industry events and parties to those raw underground showcases, LA's music hustle is fast-paced and all about connections. Eddie Caldwell has always played this city smart, knowing that whether you're looking to get signed, land a major sync deal, or link up with other artists, having the right moves in LA's music industry is what'll set you up for long-term success.

Understanding the Culture of LA's Music Industry

The Importance of Relationships in LA

In Los Angeles, the old adage "It's not what you know, but who you know" rings true. The music industry in LA thrives on personal connections and relationships. While talent is necessary, networking and building relationships with the right people are essential for opening doors to new opportunities.

- **The Power of Networking**: Unlike many other cities, LA operates largely on relationships and reputation. Every event, party, or showcase you attend is a chance to make a connection that could lead to your next big opportunity. Whether you're talking to a fellow artist, a producer, or a music supervisor, your ability to network effectively can be the difference between staying stagnant or moving forward in your career.

- **A City Built on Collaboration**: LA's music industry is deeply collaborative, and this is reflected in its culture. Artists, producers, songwriters, and industry professionals often come together to work on projects, write songs, and create opportunities. Being open to collaboration and cross-genre partnerships is vital if you want to thrive in the city's music scene.

Understanding the LA Hustle

LA is known for its fast-paced, competitive nature. It's a city full of dreamers, and the competition is fierce. To succeed, you need to embrace the hustle and be willing to work hard—often outside your comfort zone.

Do You Know? *Do you know that Los Angeles is home to over 30% of the world's music publishing, record label, and sync licensing companies? From industry mixers to underground showcases, LA is a hub where meaningful connections with industry executives and influencers can lead to collaborations and career-defining moments.*

- **Staying Ready**: Opportunities can arise at any moment, whether it's a last-minute gig, an impromptu writing session, or an introduction to a key industry player. Always be prepared with your elevator pitch, updated music portfolio, and a positive, go-getter attitude. Success in LA often comes down to being in the right place at the right time, and making the most of those moments.

- **Persistence Is Key**: You'll likely face rejection and setbacks, but persistence is essential. The music industry is full of ups and downs, and LA is no exception. Keep pushing forward, honing your craft, and expanding your network. Many of the most successful artists in LA faced multiple rejections before landing their big break.

Embracing the Unique Diversity of the LA Scene

LA's music scene is incredibly diverse, encompassing every genre from pop and hip-hop to indie rock and electronic. This diversity provides endless opportunities for collaboration and inspiration, but it also means you need to stand out and carve your own niche.

- **Find Your Community**: Within LA's vast music landscape, there are sub-scenes and communities where you can find like-minded artists and professionals. Whether it's hip-hop collectives in Leimert Park or indie rock circles in Echo Park, finding a community that aligns with your sound and goals can give you the support you need as you navigate the industry.

Tips for Navigating Industry Mixers, Parties, and Underground Showcases

Industry Mixers: Building Your Network

Industry mixers are one of the best ways to meet professionals in the music industry, from A&R reps to music supervisors, and other artists. These events are often informal but can lead to significant opportunities if you play your cards right.

- **Be Prepared with Your Elevator Pitch**: At an industry mixer, you might only have a few moments to make an impression. Be ready with a concise, compelling elevator pitch about who you are as an artist and what you're working on. Avoid coming across as overly aggressive or "thirsty"—LA is a city where being too pushy can hurt your chances. Instead, focus on having natural, authentic conversations that build rapport.

- **Bring Business Cards or Digital Contact Info**: While it might feel a bit old-school, having a business card can still be useful in the LA music scene. However, many professionals in the industry now prefer digital business cards or easy-to-access links to your social media,

website, or music portfolio. Make sure your contact information is professional and easy to share.

- **Listen More Than You Speak**: Networking isn't just about promoting yourself—it's also about listening and learning from others. Ask thoughtful questions, show genuine interest in the work of others, and be open to new ideas and collaborations. People are more likely to remember you if you engage in meaningful conversations rather than just talking about yourself.

Parties: Navigating Social Events Like a Pro

Industry parties are a regular part of the LA music scene, and while they're often casual and fun, they're also opportunities to build relationships with key figures in the industry. Unlike formal mixers, parties can be trickier to navigate because the atmosphere is more relaxed, and the line between business and socializing is often blurred.

- **Strike the Right Balance Between Fun and Business**: At parties, it's important to blend in and enjoy the atmosphere, but don't forget why you're there—to build connections. Approach people naturally, without being too business-focused right away. Find common ground, whether it's music, art, or even LA life, and let the conversation flow before steering it toward your work.

- **Don't Drink Too Much**: While many people at industry parties will be drinking, it's important to stay in control. You want to be remembered for your talent and professionalism, not for being the person who had one too many drinks. Pace yourself, stay sharp, and be aware of your surroundings. There's always the chance that an important industry player could be nearby, and first impressions matter.

- **Be Where You Need to Be, But Don't Overstay**: In LA, timing is everything. Arrive at events when they're getting started but don't feel the need to stay until the end. Knowing when to leave can be just as important as knowing when to show up. Leave while you're still at

your best—this leaves a positive impression and ensures that the connections you make are strong and professional.

Underground Showcases: Where the Magic Happens

While high-profile showcases and festivals get a lot of attention, LA is also known for its underground music scene. Underground showcases, often in smaller venues or unconventional spaces, can be a goldmine for emerging artists looking to make a name for themselves. These events are attended by a mix of passionate fans, fellow artists, and sometimes industry insiders looking to discover new talent.

- **Scout the Right Showcases**: Not all underground showcases are created equal. Research the venues and organizers to ensure that the event aligns with your style and target audience. Many showcases are genre-specific or catered to a particular type of crowd, so it's important to choose ones that fit your music and vibe.

- **Bring Your Best Performance, Every Time**: At underground showcases, you never know who's in the crowd. It could be a music supervisor scouting for fresh talent or a record label executive looking for the next big thing. Treat every showcase like it's your big break and give 100%, whether you're playing for 50 people or 500.

- **Network with Fellow Performers**: These events are prime opportunities to connect with other artists who are in the same stage of their career. Don't see them as competition—see them as potential collaborators. After the show, take the time to introduce yourself to other performers, exchange contact information, and discuss future collaborations.

Follow Up Is Crucial

Regardless of where you meet someone—whether it's an industry mixer, party, or underground showcase—the follow-up is critical. After making a connection, send a brief, personalized message within 24-48 hours. Keep

it professional, thank them for their time, and mention something specific from your conversation to help jog their memory.

- **Use Social Media for Follow-Up**: Social media is a powerful tool for staying connected after meeting someone in person. Follow them on Instagram, LinkedIn, or Twitter and engage with their content thoughtfully. This helps you stay on their radar without being too pushy. A simple comment or like on their posts shows that you're supportive and interested in maintaining the connection.

Final Thoughts: Mastering LA's Music Scene

Navigating the LA music scene requires more than just talent—it requires adaptability, persistence, and a keen understanding of the culture. By building genuine relationships, attending the right events, and knowing how to network without overwhelming people, you can unlock the doors to new opportunities. Whether you're at a formal industry mixer or an underground showcase, each interaction has the potential to move your career forward. Stay focused, stay ready, and most importantly, be yourself. With the right approach, LA's music scene can become the platform that launches your career to the next level.

3.2 Networking in LA

Networking runs the LA music scene—sometimes who you know gets you further than just talent alone. Whether you're chopping it up with execs at industry mixers, vibing with influencers at events, or linking up with other artists at showcases, the way you move can shape your whole career. But networking in LA? It's got its own rules, and if you want to stand out in a sea of talent, you gotta know how to play the game right.

How to Network Effectively with Executives and Influencers

Understanding the LA Networking Culture

Networking in LA is more about building genuine relationships than making immediate transactions. Unlike some industries where hard pitches and business card exchanges dominate, LA's music industry places a premium on forming personal connections first. Industry executives, influencers, and fellow artists are constantly approached by people looking for opportunities, so finding the right balance between professionalism and authenticity is crucial.

- **Lead with Authenticity**: LA's music scene values creativity and originality, so trying too hard to impress can come off as insincere. Instead, be yourself, and focus on building a rapport. Whether you're talking to an A&R rep, a music supervisor, or a high-profile influencer, they'll respond better to genuine conversations than a blatant attempt to network. Remember, people are more likely to help you if they like you and see you as more than just another person trying to "make it."

- **Find Common Ground**: When networking with industry professionals or influencers, look for shared interests or mutual

acquaintances as a way to build rapport. This could be anything from a shared love of a certain genre or artist to a common friend or event you both attended. These personal connections make conversations flow more naturally and can lay the foundation for future opportunities.

- **Listen More, Talk Less**: A common mistake in networking is focusing too much on yourself. Instead, ask thoughtful questions about the person's work, projects, or experiences. Show genuine interest in their career and achievements. By listening more, you can better understand their needs and see where your skills and talents may align.

Research Your Targets Beforehand

If you know you'll be attending an event where key executives or influencers will be present, do your homework. Understand who they are, what projects they're currently working on, and how your work might intersect with their needs.

- **Know Their Work**: Before approaching someone, make sure you're familiar with their background. For example, if they're a music supervisor who specializes in indie films, be ready to discuss how your sound aligns with that niche. Showing that you've done your research not only demonstrates professionalism but also shows that you're serious about making meaningful connections.

> *Your network is your net worth."* – *Porter Gale*

- **Follow Them on Social Media**: Many execs and influencers are active on social media, especially platforms like Instagram, LinkedIn, and Twitter. Follow them and engage with their content in a thoughtful, non-intrusive way. When you eventually meet them in person, this can serve as a natural icebreaker—mentioning a recent post or project they shared demonstrates that you're tuned in to their work and care about what they're doing.

Approach with a Purpose

When networking, always have a clear purpose for the conversation without being too forward or transactional. This balance is key in LA, where people are bombarded with pitches and requests daily. Your goal should be to plant seeds for future collaboration or connection, rather than to close a deal on the spot.

- **Be Specific About What You Offer**: Know what makes you stand out and what value you can bring to the table. When speaking to an executive, be ready to articulate how your music, skills, or vision can fit into the projects or business they're working on. For influencers, think about how a collaboration could be mutually beneficial—don't just focus on what you can gain from the partnership.

- **Ask for Advice, Not Favors**: When networking, especially with higher-level execs, it's often more effective to ask for advice than to directly pitch a favor. This shows respect for their experience and position and can lead to a more productive conversation. It's also more likely to foster a mentor-mentee dynamic, which could benefit you in the long run.

Perfecting Your Elevator Pitch

An elevator pitch is a short, persuasive introduction to who you are, what you do, and why the person you're talking to should care. In LA, where you may only have a few moments to make an impression, having a solid

elevator pitch can be a game-changer. But crafting one that feels authentic and avoids the hard-sell approach can be tricky.

Keep It Concise and Focused

The key to an effective elevator pitch is brevity. You should be able to communicate who you are and what you do in about 30 seconds. Any longer, and you risk losing the person's attention.

- **Start with a Strong Hook**: Your pitch should begin with something attention-grabbing that clearly communicates your identity as an artist or professional. For example, instead of saying, "I'm a musician," you could say, "I'm a songwriter who blends electronic beats with soulful vocals to create tracks perfect for film and TV soundtracks." This gives a clearer picture of what you do and positions you in a niche.

- **Focus on Your Unique Value Proposition**: What makes you different from every other artist or professional in LA? Highlight your unique strengths, whether it's your genre-blending style, your success in sync placements, or your ability to perform live and produce in the studio. Tailor your value proposition to the person you're speaking to, ensuring it aligns with their work or needs.

- **End with a Call to Action**: After delivering your pitch, offer a next step that's easy for the other person to take. This could be as simple as exchanging business cards, setting up a meeting, or following each other on social media. Don't overwhelm them with too many requests—keep it simple and professional.

Practice, but Stay Flexible

While you should rehearse your elevator pitch to make sure it's concise and clear, it's important to avoid sounding robotic. The key is to be

conversational and adaptable. Depending on who you're talking to, you might need to adjust your pitch to fit the flow of the conversation.

- **Tailor Your Pitch**: Your elevator pitch should be flexible enough to adapt to different audiences. For example, if you're speaking with an executive in the film industry, you might focus more on how your music aligns with film scores or sync placements. If you're talking to an influencer, you might emphasize your potential for collaborations or social media engagement.

- **Stay Authentic**: Even though you've practiced your pitch, remember to keep it natural. The last thing you want is to sound like you're reading off a script. Inject your personality into the pitch, and let it feel like part of the conversation rather than a rehearsed speech.

Avoiding Common Networking Pitfalls

While networking can open doors, it's easy to make mistakes that could hinder your progress. Avoiding these common pitfalls will help you make the most of every networking opportunity in LA.

Don't Be Overly Aggressive

One of the biggest mistakes you can make in LA's networking scene is being too pushy. No one wants to feel like they're being sold to, especially at informal events like mixers or parties. Networking should feel like a natural conversation, not a hard sell.

- **Avoid the "Me-Me-Me" Approach**: While it's important to talk about yourself, don't dominate the conversation with self-promotion. Be genuinely interested in what the other person has to say. Ask questions about their work, show enthusiasm for their projects, and find ways to add value to the conversation.

- **Don't Overstay Your Welcome**: Whether at a party, mixer, or event, know when to exit the conversation. If the conversation starts to feel forced or the person is looking to move on, politely end it and thank them for their time. Lingering too long can leave a negative impression.

Don't Forget to Follow Up

Making a great connection at a networking event means little if you don't follow up. Failing to follow up on a conversation or connection can lead to missed opportunities.

- **Send a Personalized Follow-Up**: After meeting someone, send a brief, personalized message within 24-48 hours. Reference something specific from your conversation to help jog their memory and express your appreciation for their time. This simple gesture can keep the connection alive and pave the way for future opportunities.

- **Use Social Media to Stay Connected**: Social media is a valuable tool for maintaining connections after in-person meetings. Follow the people you meet on platforms like LinkedIn, Instagram, or Twitter, and engage with their content thoughtfully. This keeps you on their radar without being too intrusive.

Final Thoughts: Networking with Purpose

Networking in LA's music industry is an art form, requiring a mix of authenticity, confidence, and strategic thinking. By building genuine relationships, perfecting your elevator pitch, and avoiding common pitfalls, you can effectively navigate the city's networking landscape and create opportunities that propel your career forward. Stay focused, be yourself, and always lead with the intention of adding value to every interaction. With the right approach, your network can become one of your most powerful assets in LA.

3.3 The Unspoken Rules of LA

Navigating the LA music game is like walking a tightrope—it's not just about talent and who you know, but also about mastering the city's vibe. There's more to it than what people say out loud; there are unspoken rules and social codes that can make or break how the industry sees you. Knowing how to move in these spaces helps you dodge rookie mistakes and sets you up for the long haul in this cutthroat scene.

Understanding the Etiquette and Subtle Do's and Don'ts of the LA Music Scene

1. Don't Be "Thirsty"

In LA, ambition is expected, but desperation is not. The term "thirsty" is often used to describe someone who is overly eager to get ahead—whether it's by pushing their music too hard, aggressively seeking connections, or constantly asking for favors. The key is to balance drive with tact, showing that you're hungry for success without coming off as desperate.

- **Do Be Confident, But Not Overbearing**: Confidence is essential, but there's a fine line between confidence and overconfidence. When you're at industry events, showcases, or parties, introduce yourself and talk about your work, but don't turn every conversation into a sales pitch. Let your work and personality speak for themselves without forcing it.

- **Don't Over-Promote**: It can be tempting to push your latest single or mixtape on everyone you meet, but resist the urge to hand out your links, CDs, or social media handles to every person you talk to.

Instead, let the conversation flow naturally, and if they ask to hear more about your music, then share your information. Be selective and strategic about when and how you promote your work.

2. Be Mindful of Time and Space

In LA, people are always busy and balancing multiple projects. Time is seen as one of the most valuable commodities, so respecting other people's time is key to building positive relationships.

- **Do Keep Conversations Brief**: Whether you're meeting someone at a mixer, party, or backstage at a show, keep initial conversations short and to the point. While it's important to introduce yourself and build rapport, don't dominate their time. If there's a connection, you can always follow up later to continue the conversation.

- **Don't Linger at the Wrong Moment**: Whether it's after an event or at a party, if someone seems ready to move on from a conversation or is clearly engaged with others, don't try to force more interaction. Knowing when to exit a conversation gracefully is just as important as knowing when to start one. Thank them for their time and move on—leaving on a good note ensures you'll be remembered positively.

3. Learn the Power of Follow-Up

LA is full of events and networking opportunities, but what separates those who succeed from those who don't is the ability to follow up effectively. Building a connection is only the first step; nurturing that relationship is where the real value lies.

- **Do Follow Up, But Don't Be Overly Persistent**: If you make a good connection with someone, follow up with a message or email within 24 to 48 hours. Keep it brief, polite, and specific. Mention something from your conversation to jog their memory and express interest in staying connected. If they don't respond right away, don't bombard them with more messages. A gentle follow-up after a week or two is fine, but more than that can come off as pushy.

- **Don't Ask for Too Much Too Soon**: After making a connection, avoid asking for favors or opportunities right away. Build the relationship over time, and when it feels right, present any collaborative ideas or requests. Remember, LA's music industry is built on relationships, and those take time to develop. Asking for too much too soon can burn bridges before they're fully built.

4. Always Be Professional–Even in Casual Settings

One of the quirks of the LA music scene is the blend of professionalism and casualness. It's not uncommon to have serious business discussions at parties, rooftop mixers, or even beach gatherings. While the atmosphere may be laid-back, it's important to remember that you're still in a professional space.

- **Do Dress for the Occasion, But Keep It Authentic**: LA's music industry embraces individuality, so you don't need to wear a suit and tie to impress, but you should still look put-together. Dress in a way that reflects your personal style and the vibe of the event you're attending. Whether it's a showcase or a casual industry mixer, your appearance should be authentic to your brand while still showing that you take the event seriously.

- **Don't Get Too Comfortable Too Quickly**: Even though LA can feel relaxed, always maintain a level of professionalism,

> ***Do You Know?*** *Do you know that many deals in LA are made informally, often at social gatherings, parties, and informal meetings? Learning the unspoken etiquette of the LA music scene can make or break your first impression, and knowing how to read the room is a skill that will serve you well in this industry.*

especially when interacting with industry executives or influencers. Don't overshare personal details or act too casually, especially if you're in the early stages of building a relationship. While it's fine to be yourself, you also want to project maturity and reliability.

5. The Social Media Game

Social media plays a huge role in the LA music scene. It's often the first place people go to learn more about you, and it's an important tool for staying connected with industry contacts. However, there are unwritten rules for how to engage with people online, especially if they're high-profile execs or influencers.

- **Do Engage Thoughtfully**: If you've recently met someone, follow them on social media and engage with their content—like their posts, comment when it's appropriate, and show support for their work. This keeps you on their radar in a subtle, non-intrusive way.

- **Don't Oversaturate Their Feeds**: Avoid constantly tagging industry professionals or influencers in your posts unless they're directly involved with the content. Over-tagging or flooding their DMs can make you come off as unprofessional or desperate for attention. Keep your social media interactions balanced—be supportive, but don't overdo it.

6. The Unspoken Value of Discretion

Discretion is a key component of maintaining positive relationships in the LA music scene. With so many high-profile people and opportunities around, it's important to keep certain conversations and details confidential.

- **Do Keep Sensitive Information Private**: If you're in discussions about potential collaborations, sync deals, or record contracts, be mindful of who you share that information with. Trust and discretion are highly valued in LA's music industry, and leaking information prematurely can hurt your reputation.

- **Don't Name-Drop Excessively**: While it can be tempting to mention the people you've worked with or connected with, excessive name-dropping can come off as insincere or insecure. Focus on your own work and let your connections naturally emerge in conversation when relevant. If you've truly built strong relationships, they'll come to light in more meaningful ways.

7. Respect the Hustle

Everyone in LA is grinding. Whether they're just starting out or have already made a name for themselves, people are working hard to make their dreams happen. Showing respect for others' hustle is key to gaining respect yourself.

- **Do Acknowledge Others' Efforts**: When you see someone achieving something, whether it's landing a sync placement, releasing an EP, or performing at a showcase, acknowledge their success. LA's music industry thrives on mutual support, and people appreciate it when you show respect for their hard work.

- **Don't Be Dismissive**: Avoid dismissing or underestimating others' efforts or achievements. Even if someone is at a different stage of their career, everyone in LA is chasing their dreams, and being dismissive of their progress can damage your reputation. Stay humble, stay focused on your own journey, and support others along the way.

Final Thoughts: Navigating the Unwritten Rules of LA

Mastering the unspoken rules of LA's music scene is as important as honing your musical craft. By understanding the balance between professionalism and authenticity, maintaining discretion, and respecting the hustle of others, you can build meaningful relationships that help you succeed in this competitive environment. The key to thriving in LA is not just about talent and connections—it's about how you present yourself.

CHRISTOPHER
MELONI

DYLAN
McDERMOTT

LAW & ORDER
ORGANIZED CRIME

SONGS IN THIS TV SHOW IS AN EXAMPLE OF MUSIC LICENSED
BY EDDIE CALDWELL AND MUSIC OF THE SEA

4.1 The Power of Volunteering at Industry Events

In the fast lane of the music grind, breaking through sometimes feels like a never-ending hustle. Talent, networking, and always staying on your game are a must, but one move people overlook is volunteering at industry events. It's like getting a backstage pass to the business, putting you in the room where real connections happen. You get to soak up the game firsthand and position yourself for future opportunities that can shift your whole career. Whether you're an artist, producer, or trying to carve your lane in the biz, volunteering can be that underrated key that opens up career-defining doors. Eddie Caldwell has always been about finding ways to stay in the mix, and this move is one way to stay ahead of the curve.

Why Volunteering Is a Powerful Strategy for Entering the Music Industry

1. Access to Industry Insiders

Volunteering at music events, panels, and showcases provides unparalleled access to the people who make things happen in the industry. As a volunteer, you're often placed in close proximity to event organizers, industry executives, artists, and other key players. These are individuals who might otherwise be out of reach or difficult to connect with in traditional networking settings.

- **Build Personal Connections**: Volunteering gives you the opportunity to have organic conversations with industry insiders in a more casual setting. Whether you're helping set up equipment, assisting at registration, or managing backstage areas, you'll likely

cross paths with influential people. These encounters, even brief, can lead to meaningful connections that may evolve into mentorships, collaborations, or job offers.

- **Get on the Radar of Decision-Makers**: By volunteering, you place yourself in front of people who can help advance your career. Often, music executives and organizers are paying attention to the people who go above and beyond at these events. If you make a strong impression through your work ethic, professionalism, and passion, you could be remembered the next time they're looking for talent or someone to fill a role.

2. Gain Firsthand Experience and Industry Knowledge

The music industry is multifaceted, and volunteering allows you to gain practical, on-the-ground experience that you might not get elsewhere. You'll learn the ins and outs of how music events are organized, from soundchecks to managing artists, to dealing with event logistics. This behind-the-scenes experience can provide valuable insights into how the industry operates and what's expected of artists and professionals.

- **Learn Event Logistics and Operations**: By volunteering, you'll see firsthand how events are managed, what challenges arise, and how professionals in the industry solve problems in real-time. Whether it's a concert, panel discussion, or festival, you'll observe everything from handling equipment to managing crowds and ensuring smooth transitions between sets or speakers. This knowledge will serve you well, especially if you plan to organize your own shows or work in event production down the line.

- **Understand the Business Side of Music**: Volunteering at industry panels or music conferences exposes you to discussions about the business side of the music industry. You'll hear firsthand how sync deals are negotiated, how record labels scout for talent, or what it takes to get your music placed in film and TV. By being present at

these discussions, you'll gain a deeper understanding of what it takes to succeed in the industry and what opportunities are available.

3. Show Your Dedication and Work Ethic

Volunteering demonstrates a level of commitment and passion that can't be faked. It shows that you're willing to put in the time and effort to learn, contribute, and grow within the industry, even when you're not being paid for it. For artists, volunteering can also show that you're serious about understanding the business side of your career, not just the creative aspect.

- **Stand Out for Future Opportunities**: Industry professionals often appreciate people who are willing to start from the ground up. When you volunteer, you're putting yourself in a position to be noticed not just for your talents, but for your work ethic, reliability, and professionalism. These traits are highly valued in the industry, and people are more likely to recommend or hire someone who has shown dedication and initiative.

- **Create a Reputation for Being Resourceful**: Many successful people in the music industry started by volunteering or interning. By helping at events, solving problems as they arise, and staying calm under pressure, you're building a reputation as someone who can be counted on. In an industry where trust and dependability are key, this can be a huge asset.

4. Low-Pressure Networking

Volunteering offers a more relaxed environment for networking compared to formal industry mixers or showcases. Since you're working behind the scenes, the pressure is off to immediately impress someone with your resume or talent. Instead, you're contributing to the event's success, which naturally leads to conversations and interactions.

- **Form Organic Relationships**: Unlike more formal networking events, volunteering allows you to build relationships over time,

without the immediate pressure to "sell" yourself. As you work alongside industry professionals and other volunteers, you'll have more opportunities to connect naturally, leading to deeper, more meaningful relationships.

- **Expand Your Network**: In addition to meeting industry professionals, you'll also network with fellow volunteers who are often up-and-coming artists, producers, or music industry hopefuls. These peer connections can be just as valuable, as many industry collaborations and opportunities come from peers recommending each other for projects or roles.

Where to Find Opportunities to Volunteer at Music Events, Panels, and Showcases

Now that you understand the benefits of volunteering, the next step is knowing where to find opportunities. Luckily, in a city like Los Angeles, and even in smaller music hubs around the world, there are plenty of events looking for passionate, reliable volunteers.

1. Music Festivals

Large music festivals, such as Coachella, SXSW, and Lollapalooza, often rely on volunteers to help manage logistics, artist relations, and event operations. These festivals are attended by major industry players, making them prime opportunities to build connections while gaining experience.

- **How to Volunteer**: Most festivals have volunteer application sections on their websites. Be sure to apply early, as spots can fill up fast. Look for roles that align with your interests or career goals—whether it's working in artist relations, event production, or stage management.

2. Music Conferences and Panels

Music conferences such as ASCAP's "I Create Music" Expo, SyncSummit, MUSEXPO, and Billboard's "Music Week" are rich with opportunities to volunteer. These events are centered around industry knowledge-sharing, networking, and showcasing new talent, making them ideal places to get face time with executives, music supervisors, and established artists.

> *"Volunteering is the ultimate exercise in democracy. You vote in elections once a year, but when you volunteer, you vote every day about the kind of community you want to live in." – Marjorie Moore*

- **How to Volunteer**: Check the official websites of these conferences for volunteer applications. Many events are looking for help with registration, panel coordination, and general event support. Volunteering here not only gives you access to the panels and discussions but also offers opportunities to meet and assist high-profile attendees.

3. Showcases and Industry Mixers

Local music showcases, whether they're in cities like LA, New York, or Austin, provide opportunities for emerging artists and industry hopefuls to get involved. These events are typically smaller and more intimate, offering a chance to meet local talent, producers, and event organizers.

- **How to Volunteer**: Local venues and event promoters often post calls for volunteers on social media or through their websites. Reach out to event organizers directly, offering your help with things like setup, soundcheck assistance, or guest management. You'll get to know the key players in your local music scene and possibly meet industry reps scouting for talent.

4. Non-Profit Music Organizations

There are several non-profit organizations focused on music education, artist advocacy, and industry mentorship that rely heavily on volunteers. Groups like the Grammy Foundation, MusicCares, and Little Kids Rock

host events and panels that often need volunteers to help organize and manage logistics.

- **How to Volunteer**: Visit the websites of these organizations and inquire about volunteer opportunities. These types of organizations are often involved with industry events and have strong connections with established artists and professionals, providing a direct line to networking and experience.

5. Independent Showcases and Artist Collective Events

Indie artist collectives, such as those that host underground showcases or music pop-ups, often rely on volunteers to help run events. These smaller, community-focused events are great for networking with other emerging artists, managers, and music producers.

- **How to Volunteer**: Follow local artist collectives, indie music blogs, and event organizers on social media. Many of these collectives are looking for volunteers to help with event promotion, ticketing, and logistics. Getting involved with grassroots movements can give you a deeper understanding of the music scene and build close-knit relationships with rising talent.

Final Thoughts: Volunteering as Your Pathway into the Music Industry

Volunteering at industry events, panels, and showcases is one of the smartest strategies for gaining access to the music industry. It allows you to build relationships with key players, gain invaluable experience, and demonstrate your dedication and work ethic—all without the immediate pressure of needing to impress. Whether you're looking to get your foot in the door or gain insider knowledge, volunteering can offer the opportunities you need to move your career forward. So, find the events that align with your goals, offer your time, and start building the foundation for your future in music.

4.2 How Volunteering Can Lead to Big Breaks

Volunteering in the music game ain't just about clocking hours—it's your ticket to real opportunities, the kind that could set you up for long-term wins. A lot of the big names you know—artists, execs, and movers in the industry—started by grinding as volunteers. They took that hustle and flipped it into major moves. In this section, Eddie Caldwell is gonna break down real stories of folks who turned their volunteer work into game-changers, and he'll drop gems on how you can make the most of your time in the trenches, learning from the pros while you're at it.

Real-Life Stories of Individuals Who Turned Volunteer Gigs into Long-Term Success

1. Scooter Braun: From Event Promoter to Industry Mogul

Scooter Braun, one of the most successful music executives today, started his career as a volunteer promoter. Braun began promoting parties and events while attending college, which gave him the opportunity to build relationships with musicians, event organizers, and industry insiders. By volunteering his time and energy, he quickly built a network that would eventually lead him to discover and manage Justin Bieber.

- **Key Takeaway**: Braun's success shows how volunteering can lead to valuable connections. By positioning himself at the center of industry events and offering value to those around him, he was able to make himself indispensable. His proactive approach and willingness to put in extra effort ultimately led to his role as one of the most influential figures in music today.

2. Jennifer Venditti: From Volunteer to Talent Scout

Jennifer Venditti, a celebrated casting director and producer, started her career by volunteering at fashion shows and events. While working behind the scenes, she developed a keen eye for talent, and her dedication didn't go unnoticed. Her volunteer work led to opportunities to scout talent for fashion shoots, which eventually led her into the world of film and music videos. Venditti's ability to spot unique talent helped her transition from a volunteer to a sought-after professional in the casting world.

- **Key Takeaway**: Venditti's story illustrates how volunteering can help you hone your skills and get noticed by industry professionals. By actively participating and showcasing your unique talents, you can attract attention and eventually be offered more significant responsibilities.

3. Diplo: From DJ to Global Superstar

Before Diplo became an internationally renowned DJ and producer, he spent time volunteering at music festivals and underground events. By positioning himself in the right spaces, he was able to meet key influencers in the electronic music scene and build his reputation as a DJ. His volunteer gigs allowed him to network with other artists, gain exposure, and eventually land higher-profile gigs that led to his breakout success.

- **Key Takeaway**: Diplo's journey emphasizes the importance of persistence and presence. Volunteering allowed him to immerse himself in the music community, where he built relationships that would later lead to larger opportunities. His willingness to put in time at grassroots events paid off when he transitioned into mainstream success.

4. Tiffany Gaines: From Intern to Entrepreneur

Tiffany Gaines, CEO of SS Global Entertainment, started her career by volunteering at industry events and internships for record labels. Through volunteering, she made key connections with artists, managers, and label

executives. Gaines used these connections and the knowledge she gained to start her own management company, which now oversees the careers of over 4,000 artists.

- **Key Takeaway**: Gaines's story highlights how volunteering and interning can provide you with the knowledge and contacts needed to build your own business. By taking the initiative to learn and network through volunteer opportunities, she was able to transition from volunteer gigs to becoming a successful entrepreneur in the music industry.

How to Maximize Your Exposure and Learn from Industry Pros While Volunteering

Volunteering at industry events can be your entry point into the music world, but it's important to approach these opportunities strategically. Here are some ways to maximize your exposure and learn from industry professionals while volunteering.

1. Be Proactive and Show Initiative

When you're volunteering, don't just do the bare minimum—go above and beyond. Industry professionals value individuals who take initiative and demonstrate a strong work ethic. If you see a task that needs to be done, step up and offer to help, even if it's outside your assigned role.

Take on Leadership Roles: If you're volunteering at an event and there's a need for someone to lead or organize a task, step forward. This can set you apart from other volunteers and put you in direct contact with the event's organizers and decision-makers.

- **Solve Problems**: Event organizers and industry professionals appreciate volunteers who can think on their feet. If a problem arises during an event—whether it's technical issues or logistical hiccups— help find a solution. Problem-solving shows that you're reliable and resourceful, which can lead to more opportunities down the road.

Do You Know? *Do you know that volunteering positions often lead to full-time roles or key industry connections? Many professionals started their careers as unpaid volunteers, using the opportunity to build relationships and learn from seasoned industry leaders. Persistence and a positive attitude can turn small gigs into big breaks.*

2. Network Smartly, Not Aggressively

While volunteering gives you proximity to industry professionals, it's important to approach networking with care. Instead of bombarding people with your pitch, focus on building genuine connections. Take advantage of the informal environment of volunteering to have organic conversations with those around you.

- **Be Observant and Strategic**: Watch for the right moments to introduce yourself. If an industry professional is busy managing a crisis or focused on the event, hold back. Find a time when things are more relaxed to approach them, introduce yourself, and express interest in their work.

- **Make a Positive Impression**: Your work ethic will speak volumes, but when you do have the opportunity to talk to industry pros, keep it concise and professional. Mention that you're interested in learning more about their work, and be ready to follow up with them after the event. Leave a lasting impression by being polite, helpful, and respectful of their time.

3. Learn Through Observation

One of the greatest benefits of volunteering is the chance to learn from those who are already successful in the industry. While working at events,

take the time to observe how professionals interact, handle challenges, and navigate the music industry.

- **Watch Industry Pros in Action**: Whether it's how an artist handles a performance, how a music supervisor picks tracks for a film, or how event organizers manage logistics, pay close attention to what works and what doesn't. These lessons can be invaluable when it comes to your own career, giving you insights into how to succeed in various facets of the industry.

- **Ask Questions When Appropriate**: If the opportunity arises, don't be afraid to ask questions. Industry professionals often appreciate curiosity, especially from volunteers who are eager to learn. However, be mindful of their time and avoid asking questions during high-pressure moments. Instead, wait for lulls in the action to engage in meaningful conversations.

4. Follow Up and Stay Connected

After volunteering, the work isn't over. Following up with the connections you made is crucial for turning a one-time experience into a long-term relationship. Whether it's a brief email, a social media message, or a formal thank-you note, following up can keep you on the radar of industry professionals.

- **Send Personalized Follow-Ups**: Don't send generic emails. Mention something specific about the event or conversation you had to remind them who you are and show that you were paying attention. A simple "It was great meeting you at [event]—I really enjoyed our conversation about [specific topic]" can go a long way in fostering future opportunities.

- **Keep in Touch**: Staying connected doesn't mean constantly emailing or messaging the people you met. Instead, engage with their social media, show support for their projects, and be present when future opportunities arise. Staying visible in a respectful way keeps you in their minds when new opportunities become available.

5. Use Every Experience to Build Your Portfolio

Even if you're volunteering, treat every experience as a professional opportunity to build your portfolio. Take notes, document your work (if appropriate), and use your volunteer experiences as learning tools for future opportunities.

- **Highlight Key Achievements**: Whether you were responsible for managing artist relations, helping with soundcheck, or assisting in event organization, highlight these skills in your resume or portfolio. Employers in the music industry value hands-on experience, and your volunteer work can demonstrate that you have the practical knowledge to succeed in the field.

Final Thoughts: Volunteering as a Pathway to Success

Volunteering can be your golden ticket to success in the music industry, as demonstrated by the real-life stories of professionals who started their careers by offering their time and skills. By taking a proactive approach, networking thoughtfully, and following up strategically, you can maximize your exposure, learn from industry pros, and turn volunteer gigs into long-term opportunities. Whether you're looking to make connections, gain experience, or learn from the best, volunteering is a powerful and often overlooked tool for advancing your music career.

MUSIC OF THE SEA
Emmy Nominated Shows

CONGRATULATIONS!!

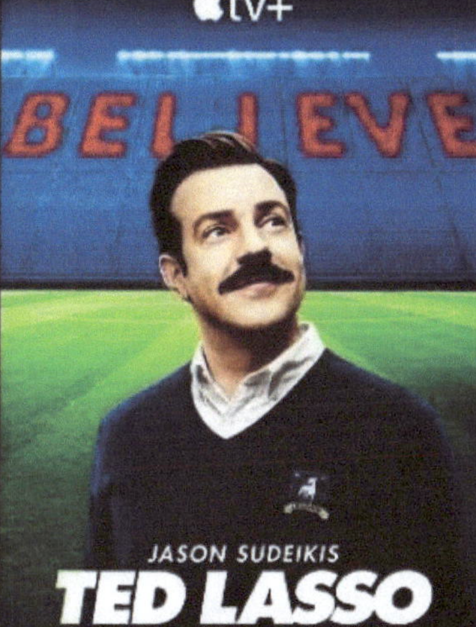

SONGS IN THESE FILMS AND SHOWS ARE EXAMPLES OF MUSIC LICENSED BY EDDIE CALDWELL AND MUSIC OF THE SEA

5.1 Choosing the Right Collaborators

Collaboration is a serious cheat code when it comes to leveling up your music game. Bringing in new energy and fresh ideas can really take your sound to the next level. But here's the deal—you gotta pick your people wisely. Whether it's artists, producers, or songwriters, the crew you roll with should elevate your vibe, not water it down. The best collabs hit that sweet spot between being creative and handling the business side like a pro. In this section, Eddie Caldwell is gonna break down how to find the right people who match your sound and how to handle your business while working with them.

How to Identify Artists and Producers Who Complement Your Sound

1. Know Your Own Sound First

Before you can identify collaborators who complement your style, it's important to have a deep understanding of your own sound. This involves not just knowing your genre, but also your unique artistic identity, influences, and the message you want to convey through your music. Collaborations are most successful when there's a strong foundation to build on, so take time to clarify your strengths, weaknesses, and artistic goals.

- **Identify Your Core Identity**: Are you an artist who focuses on emotional storytelling, energetic performances, or experimental sounds? Understanding your core identity helps you find collaborators who can enhance your strengths rather than overpower or divert from them.

- **Define Your Long-Term Vision**: What are your goals for the next stage of your music career? Whether it's expanding your sound, breaking into a new market, or landing more sync deals, knowing where you're headed will help you align with collaborators who can help you reach those goals.

> *"Coming together is a beginning, staying together is progress, and working together is success."*
>
> *– Henry Ford*

2. Look for Complementary Strengths

One of the best things about collaboration is that it allows you to benefit from the strengths of others. The ideal collaborator is someone who brings something new to the table without clashing with your artistic vision. Whether it's a producer who has expertise in a genre you're exploring or a featured artist whose style complements yours, it's essential to find people whose strengths complement your sound.

- **Complement, Don't Duplicate**: When seeking collaborators, avoid those who do exactly what you do. Instead, look for artists or producers who offer a fresh perspective or skill set that enhances your music. For instance, if you're a singer-songwriter focused on acoustic sounds, working with a producer who specializes in electronic or ambient music can create something uniquely innovative.

- **Consider Genre Crossovers**: Some of the most exciting collaborations happen when artists from different genres come together. Think of collaborations like Beyoncé and Jack White or Post

Malone and Ozzy Osbourne—pairings that seemed unexpected but resulted in fresh, genre-defying tracks. Look for collaborators who might push you outside your comfort zone while still aligning with your broader creative goals.

3. Evaluate Professional Compatibility

Artistic chemistry is essential, but professional compatibility is equally important. You need collaborators who share your work ethic, approach to deadlines, and commitment to the project. Creative collaborations can fall apart if one person is unreliable or has a vastly different approach to professionalism.

- **Check Their Track Record**: Look into the potential collaborator's past work and reputation. Have they been reliable and easy to work with in previous projects? Do they meet deadlines, communicate clearly, and handle the business side of music with care? Professionalism matters just as much as creativity, especially if the collaboration involves significant investments of time and resources.

- **Mutual Respect for Boundaries**: Healthy collaboration requires clear boundaries, both creative and professional. Ensure that your potential collaborator respects your vision and boundaries and that you respect theirs. Setting expectations about how decisions will be made and how responsibilities will be divided early on can prevent conflicts later.

4. Start Small if Necessary

If you're unsure about a long-term collaboration, it's perfectly fine to start with a smaller project before committing to something larger. This could be co-writing a single song, producing one track, or even experimenting with a remix. By starting small, you can gauge how well your creative and professional processes align.

- **Test the Waters**: Consider inviting a potential collaborator to work on a single track or even remix one of your existing songs. This low-stakes project can help you understand their creative style, work ethic, and whether the chemistry is there for a more in-depth collaboration.

- **Evaluate the Collaboration**: After working together on a smaller project, take time to evaluate the experience. Was the communication smooth? Did the collaboration enhance your sound? If the project was successful and enjoyable, it's a good sign that you can move forward with larger, more ambitious collaborations.

Balancing Creativity with the Business Side of Collaboration

Collaboration doesn't just involve creative synergy—it also requires careful management of the business aspects. Contracts, royalty splits, and clear communication about expectations are key to ensuring that both parties benefit from the collaboration and that the project runs smoothly from start to finish.

1. Clearly Define Roles and Responsibilities

Before diving into a collaboration, it's crucial to define who is responsible for what. This not only helps manage creative expectations but also clarifies the practical elements of the collaboration, such as who will handle production, distribution, promotion, or financial contributions.

- **Creative Contributions**: Will both parties contribute equally to songwriting and production? If one person is handling more of the creative workload, such as producing all of the beats or writing most of the lyrics, make sure these contributions are acknowledged in both credits and compensation.

- **Business Responsibilities**: Clarify who will handle the business side of things, such as coordinating studio time, managing release schedules, or promoting the project. Ensuring that all responsibilities are outlined from the start helps avoid misunderstandings and ensures that both parties are equally invested in the success of the collaboration.

2. Negotiate Royalties and Credits Early

One of the most critical aspects of a successful collaboration is transparency around how the project will be credited and how any revenue will be shared. This includes agreeing on how royalties will be split for songwriting, performance, and production, as well as making sure both parties are credited appropriately when the project is released.

- **Discuss Splits Up Front**: Before any music is made, have a clear discussion about how you'll divide royalties. Standard splits for songwriting are often 50/50, but this can change depending on who is contributing what to the project. If a producer is handling all of the production and you're handling all of the lyrics, you might split things differently. Whatever the case, ensure the agreement is documented in writing.

- **Get It in Writing**: Always formalize your agreements in writing, even if you have a close personal relationship with the collaborator. Having a contract protects both parties and ensures that the terms of the collaboration—whether it's royalty splits, credits, or timelines—are legally binding.

3. Balance Creative Input with Business Strategy

Collaboration often involves compromise, especially when two artists or producers with different creative visions come together. However, it's important to balance artistic expression with business strategy. A great collaboration can push creative boundaries while still maintaining commercial appeal and meeting the practical goals of both parties.

- **Consider Commercial Viability**: If one of your goals is to generate revenue from the collaboration—whether through streaming, licensing, or live performances—it's important to balance creativity with market appeal. Work with your collaborator to ensure that while the music remains true to your artistic vision, it also has the potential to resonate with your target audience and meet your business objectives.

- **Creative Control vs. Commercial Input**: Be clear from the start about how much creative control each party will have. If one collaborator is primarily concerned with artistic experimentation while the other is more focused on the commercial success of the project, there may be friction. Establish clear boundaries and agree on the level of creative freedom versus commercial considerations.

4. Maintain Open Communication

Communication is the key to any successful collaboration. Throughout the process, ensure that both parties feel comfortable discussing everything from creative ideas to business decisions. Open communication helps avoid misunderstandings and ensures that both sides feel valued and heard.

- **Regular Check-Ins**: Schedule regular check-ins throughout the collaboration to ensure that both parties are aligned on progress, creative direction, and business logistics. This prevents small issues from becoming major problems and helps keep the project on track.

- **Be Transparent About Concerns**: If issues arise, whether creative or logistical, address them early. Letting frustrations build up can derail a project, but dealing with concerns transparently and respectfully can keep the collaboration productive and enjoyable.

Final Thoughts: Finding the Right Balance

Choosing the right collaborators can be transformative for your career, bringing new creative energy and expanding your audience. However, it's crucial to strike a balance between creativity and the business side of collaboration. By carefully selecting collaborators who complement your sound, clearly defining roles and responsibilities, and maintaining open communication, you can ensure that your collaborations are both artistically fulfilling and professionally successful. The right collaboration can not only enhance your music but also open doors to new opportunities and long-term growth in the industry.

5.2 Why Collaborations Are Key to Sync Success

In the sync game—where your music gets placed in everything from TV shows and movies to commercials and video games—collabs are the real cheat code. The sync world craves tracks that can shift gears, stay fresh, and fit right into any scene while still standing out. When artists, producers, and songwriters link up, they blend their styles, making something unique that's built to score those big sync placements.

Like Eddie Caldwell always tells us, "You gotta mix it up, bring different flavors to the table, or you're just another track in the background." Collaboration is how you create that magic.

The Value of Versatility in Sync Music

1. Sync Music Requires a Diverse Range of Styles

One of the most significant reasons collaborations are key to sync success is that sync opportunities often require a diverse range of musical styles. Depending on the needs of the project, a song might need to evoke different emotions, cross genres, or complement specific visuals. Collaborating with others allows you to blend different elements of musical genres and create a track that is dynamic and versatile.

- **Blending Genres for Maximum Appeal**: Sync supervisors are constantly looking for tracks that stand out but also fit the scene or brand they're working with. Collaborations between artists of different genres—whether it's blending hip-hop with electronic, folk with pop, or classical with indie rock—can result in songs that are more likely to capture attention. This genre-blending versatility gives your music a greater chance of being selected.

- **Adapting to Different Emotional Tones**: Sync music needs to be adaptable to various moods and tones. Collaborations allow for a greater range of creative expression, making it easier to produce tracks that convey different emotions. For example, a collaboration between a songwriter who specializes in upbeat pop and a producer with a knack for ambient or moody soundscapes can create a track that transitions seamlessly between light and dark tones, making it perfect for different sync opportunities.

2. Collaboration Enhances Creativity and Innovation

Collaborating with other artists and producers helps foster creative innovation, which is essential in a highly competitive sync market. Sync supervisors are often looking for something fresh—music that offers a new twist or an unexpected sound. By working with collaborators who bring different skills and perspectives, you can push the boundaries of your sound and create tracks that stand out.

- **Fresh Ideas Lead to Unique Tracks**: Collaborations encourage experimentation, which can lead to the creation of tracks that are both original and commercially viable. Producers may suggest adding new elements—such as live instrumentation or digital effects—that you wouldn't have considered on your own, while vocalists or songwriters might offer lyrical perspectives or melodies that take the track in a new direction.

> *"Collaboration is the essence of life. The wind, bees, and flowers work together to spread the pollen."*
>
> *– Amit Ray*

- **Versatility Through Multiple Influences**: When multiple creative minds come together, the resulting music is often more versatile, incorporating influences from different genres, cultural backgrounds, or artistic visions. This versatility is exactly what sync supervisors are looking for because it allows the track to fit multiple contexts. A track that can evoke different emotions depending on the visuals it accompanies is a prime candidate for sync licensing.

3. Expanding Your Network and Sync Opportunities

Collaborations not only enhance your music but also expand your network and increase your chances of landing sync deals. Each collaborator brings their own contacts and connections, which can significantly widen the scope of opportunities for your music. Sync licensing is often about who you know, and collaborating with other artists or producers can introduce you to music supervisors, agencies, and other industry professionals who specialize in sync.

- **Leveraging Each Other's Connections**: By collaborating with artists or producers who have experience in sync, you can tap into their existing relationships with sync agencies, music supervisors, and media companies. This can lead to more exposure for your music and better chances of getting your tracks placed in high-profile projects.

- **Collaborating with Sync Specialists**: Some producers and artists specialize in creating music specifically for sync. Collaborating with these specialists can give you insight into what works in the sync world—everything from song structure to instrumentation to length. They can also provide valuable advice on how to tailor your music to meet the needs of sync supervisors, increasing your chances of success.

Examples of Successful Collaborations that Landed Major Sync Deals

1. Sia and David Guetta – "Titanium"

Sia's collaboration with electronic music producer David Guetta on the song "Titanium" is a perfect example of how blending different musical styles can lead to sync success. While Guetta brought his signature high-energy electronic beats, Sia's emotional and powerful vocals gave the track a depth that resonated with both radio audiences and sync supervisors. The song has been used in multiple sync placements, including trailers for movies like *Pitch Perfect* and *Battleship*.

- **Why It Worked**: The collaboration between Sia and Guetta resulted in a track that was both energetic and emotionally compelling. This versatility made it suitable for a variety of sync placements, from action-packed movie trailers to emotionally intense scenes in TV shows. The combination of anthemic production and heartfelt vocals made it a go-to track for sync supervisors looking for music that could elevate visual content.

2. The Weeknd and Daft Punk – "Starboy"

When The Weeknd teamed up with electronic duo Daft Punk, they created the smash hit "Starboy," which quickly became a favorite for sync placements. The track has been used in numerous commercials and TV shows, thanks to its sleek production, futuristic vibe, and The Weeknd's distinctive vocals. Daft Punk's electronic production style complemented The Weeknd's darker, moody sound, creating a track that stood out in the sync world.

- **Why It Worked**: The collaboration between The Weeknd and Daft Punk blended two distinctive styles—The Weeknd's sultry R&B vibe with Daft Punk's signature electronic sound. This fusion resulted in a track that was both radio-friendly and sync-friendly, with its futuristic sound making it a great fit for commercials and TV shows that wanted a cutting-edge, modern feel. The track's versatility allowed it to be used in multiple contexts, from car commercials to action-packed TV scenes.

3. Bon Iver and Kanye West – "Lost in the World"

The collaboration between indie folk artist Bon Iver and rapper Kanye West on "Lost in the World" showcased how two seemingly opposite genres can come together to create something sync-friendly and unique. The track combines Bon Iver's haunting, atmospheric sound with Kanye's signature hip-hop beats, making it a powerful and versatile song that has been used in TV shows and films.

- **Why It Worked**: The collaboration merged two distinct worlds—indie folk and hip-hop—creating a track that was fresh and innovative. Its emotional depth, combined with a modern production style, made it a compelling choice for sync placements. The song's ability to transition between introspective moments and energetic beats gave it the versatility needed for a variety of sync opportunities, from dramatic scenes to more upbeat commercials.

4. Imagine Dragons and Alex Da Kid – "Radioactive"

"Radioactive," the hit collaboration between rock band Imagine Dragons and producer Alex Da Kid, became a massive success in both the charts and the sync world. The song has been featured in everything from movie trailers to TV commercials, video games, and sporting event promotions. The track's genre-defying blend of rock, electronic elements, and powerful lyrics made it highly adaptable for different media contexts.

- **Why It Worked**: The collaboration between Imagine Dragons and Alex Da Kid resulted in a bold, cinematic track that could be used across a variety of media. Its combination of rock energy and electronic production made it dynamic enough to fit action-packed sequences, trailers, and even emotional scenes. This versatility, paired with its anthemic quality, made "Radioactive" one of the most sought-after songs for sync licensing.

Final Thoughts: Collaborations as a Key to Sync Success

Collaborations are a powerful tool for achieving sync success because they bring together different strengths, perspectives, and networks. By blending genres, pushing creative boundaries, and leveraging each other's connections, collaborations can lead to music that is not only versatile and innovative but also highly sought after by sync supervisors. As shown by the success of tracks like "Titanium," "Starboy," and "Radioactive," collaborations that balance creativity with commercial appeal are more likely to land major sync deals. When artists, producers, and songwriters come together to create music that stands out, the potential for sync success increases exponentially.

5.3 Case Studies: Collaboration Success Stories

Collabs have always been a major move in the music industry, and some of the dopest sync placements have come from artists linking up. These partnerships blend different styles and skills, cooking up tracks that are versatile, cutting-edge, and ready-made for TV, movies, commercials, and video games. In this section, Eddie Caldwell's gonna walk you through some big-time sync success stories, showing how the right collab can open the door to major breakthroughs in the sync world.

1. Beyoncé & Jack White – "Don't Hurt Yourself"

The collaboration between Beyoncé and Jack White on "Don't Hurt Yourself" from Beyoncé's *Lemonade* album is a prime example of how unexpected pairings can create powerful music that thrives in the sync world. The song combines Beyoncé's fierce vocals with Jack White's gritty, rock-infused production, creating a track with intense emotional depth and raw energy.

- **Sync Success**: "Don't Hurt Yourself" was used in HBO's promotional trailers for the show *Westworld*, a futuristic series known for its dark, dystopian themes. The intensity of the collaboration's sound made it a perfect fit for the show's high-stakes drama.

- **Why It Worked**: The contrast between Beyoncé's R&B power and Jack White's rock edge gave the track a unique sound that was both bold and emotionally charged. This collaboration produced a track that was versatile enough to be used in a wide range of media, from TV show promotions to dramatic scenes in films.

2. Post Malone & Swae Lee – "Sunflower"

Post Malone and Swae Lee's collaboration on the track "Sunflower" became one of the biggest sync success stories in recent years. The song, which features Post Malone's signature laid-back delivery and Swae Lee's melodic hooks, was created for the *Spider-Man: Into the Spider-Verse* soundtrack and became a massive hit both commercially and in sync placements.

- **Sync Success**: "Sunflower" was prominently featured in the *Spider-Man: Into the Spider-Verse* film and its promotional campaigns. The song's catchy, upbeat melody and youthful vibe made it a perfect fit for the animated superhero movie.

- **Why It Worked**: The collaboration between Post Malone and Swae Lee brought together two distinct but complementary styles—Post Malone's laid-back, genre-blurring sound and Swae Lee's melodic hip-hop. The song's feel-good vibe, coupled with its versatility, allowed it to transcend the film and become a standalone hit, used in commercials, video games, and other media.

3. The Weeknd & Daft Punk – "I Feel It Coming"

The Weeknd's collaboration with Daft Punk on the track "I Feel It Coming" is another great example of how collaborations can result in sync success. The track, which features Daft Punk's smooth electronic production combined with The Weeknd's sultry vocals, created a sound that was both retro and modern.

- **Sync Success**: "I Feel It Coming" has been featured in multiple commercials, including for major brands like Apple Music. Its smooth, laid-back sound, combined with its modern production, made it an ideal choice for tech and lifestyle brands looking for a song that resonates with a wide audience.

- **Why It Worked**: collaboration between The Weeknd and Daft Punk blended electronic and R&B elements seamlessly. The track's universal appeal, danceable rhythm, and emotional undertones made it a go-to sync choice for brands seeking

> **Do You Know?** Do you know that artists like Calvin Harris and Rihanna created multi-platinum hits through their collaboration? Major sync deals have emerged from unexpected collaborations, demonstrating that working together with the right partners can lead to mainstream success.

music that could appeal to both younger and older demographics.

4. Imagine Dragons & Kendrick Lamar – "Radioactive" (Remix)

The remix of Imagine Dragons' hit song "Radioactive" featuring Kendrick Lamar was a notable collaboration that created a powerful fusion of rock and hip-hop. The original version of "Radioactive" was already a sync favorite, thanks to its cinematic production and anthemic energy, but the remix with Kendrick Lamar took the track to another level.

- **Sync Success**: The remix was prominently used in action-packed TV shows, commercials, and trailers. Its high-energy production and Kendrick Lamar's powerful verses made it perfect for intense scenes and promotional content.

- **Why It Worked**: The collaboration combined the powerful, anthemic sound of Imagine Dragons with Kendrick Lamar's socially conscious lyrics and raw delivery. The result was a track that worked well across various media, particularly in sync placements that required both intensity and depth.

5. Run the Jewels & DJ Shadow – "Nobody Speak"

Run the Jewels' collaboration with DJ Shadow on the track "Nobody Speak" is a great example of how a powerful, genre-blending song can lead to widespread sync success. The track features a combination of Run the Jewels' aggressive, politically charged lyrics and DJ Shadow's cutting-edge production, resulting in a high-energy, rebellious anthem.

- **Sync Success**: "Nobody Speak" has been used in a variety of TV shows, films, and commercials, including the hit show *Silicon Valley* and various ad campaigns. Its punchy beat and bold lyrics made it an ideal choice for sync opportunities that wanted to evoke a rebellious, energetic tone.

- **Why It Worked**: The track's unique combination of hip-hop and electronic production made it stand out in the sync world. Its aggressive, in-your-face style perfectly suited media that required bold and powerful music to accompany high-energy or dramatic visuals.

6. Florence + The Machine & Calvin Harris – "Sweet Nothing"

The collaboration between Florence Welch of Florence + The Machine and Calvin Harris on the track "Sweet Nothing" resulted in a song that was both emotionally charged and dancefloor-ready. The track combines Welch's ethereal vocals with Harris's high-energy electronic production, creating a powerful song that was ripe for sync placement.

- **Sync Success**: "Sweet Nothing" has been used in a variety of commercials, including ads for major fashion brands and lifestyle products. Its emotional intensity, coupled with its electronic production, made it ideal for brands looking for music that felt both cinematic and modern.

- **Why It Worked**: The collaboration brought together the best of both worlds—Florence Welch's dramatic, emotionally rich vocals and Calvin Harris's danceable, electronic beats. This fusion of styles created a track that worked in both emotional and upbeat contexts, making it highly versatile for sync placements.

Final Thoughts: Collaborations as a Key to Sync Success

The success stories highlighted here demonstrate how collaborations between artists, producers, and songwriters can lead to major sync breakthroughs. By bringing together different styles, genres, and creative perspectives, these collaborations resulted in tracks that were not only commercially successful but also highly sought after for sync placements. Whether it's the genre-blending power of "Radioactive" or the emotional depth of "Sweet Nothing," these collaborations show that when artists work together, they can create music that resonates across multiple media platforms and becomes a go-to choice for sync supervisors.

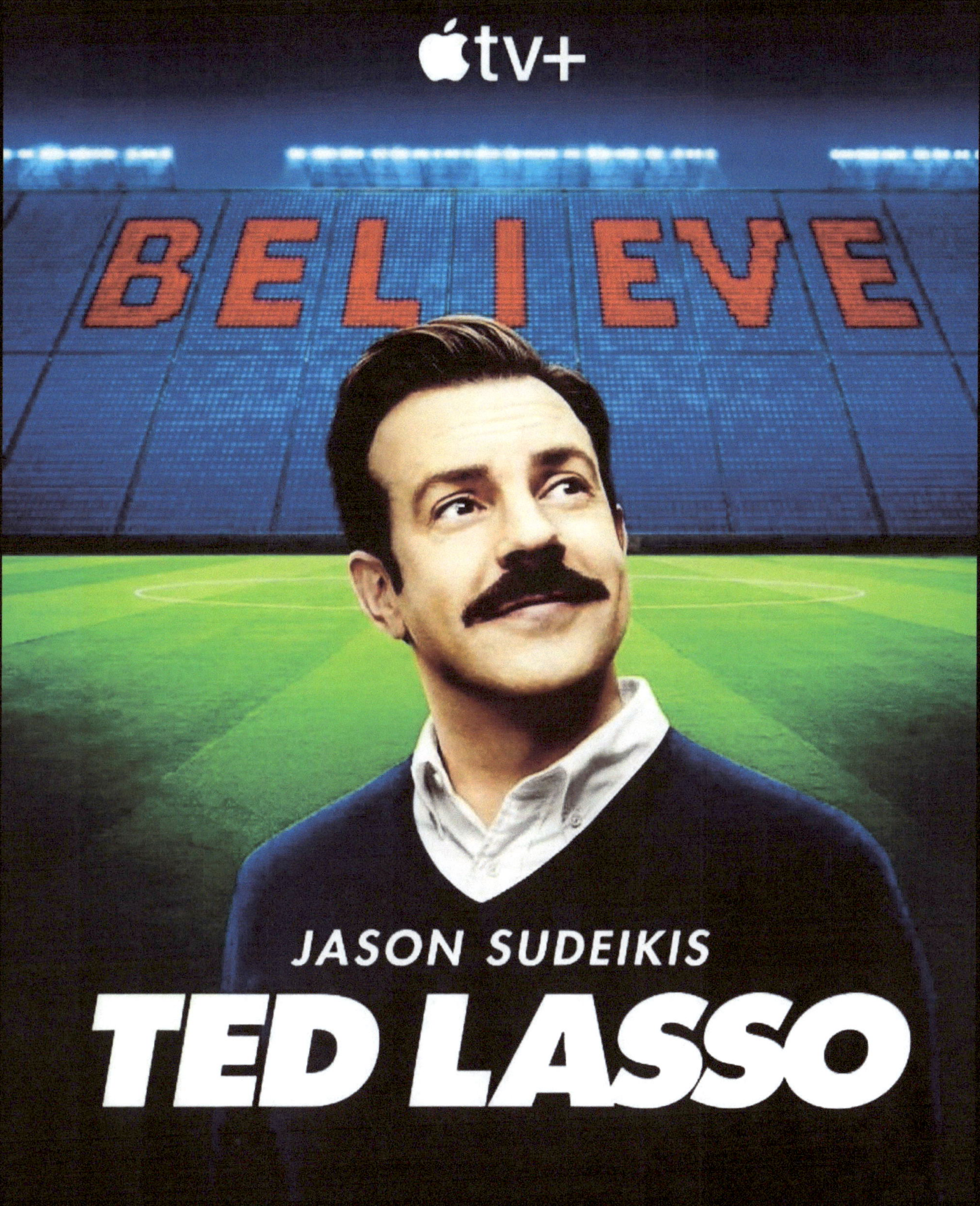

SONGS IN THIS FILM IS AN EXAMPLE OF MUSIC LICENSED BY EDDIE CALDWELL AND MUSIC OF THE SEA

6.1 The Top Music Conferences You Should Attend

Pulling up to music industry conferences is one of the best moves you can make to level up your career. These events are where the real connections happen—artists, producers, managers, A&R reps, sync supervisors, and everybody who's anybody in the business shows up. It's a spot to soak up knowledge and build relationships that can take you far. Eddie Caldwell's got the lowdown on must-hit music industry conferences and what you can gain from each one. Plus, we'll break down why these events are clutch for locking in long-term relationships that can push your career to the next level.

1. SXSW (South by Southwest) – Austin, TX

What You Can Gain

SXSW is one of the largest and most influential music conferences in the world. It offers a unique blend of music, film, and interactive media, attracting thousands of industry professionals. For musicians, it's an opportunity to showcase your work in front of influential attendees, including music supervisors, A&R reps, and festival curators. Beyond performances, SXSW features panel discussions, workshops, and networking events that cover every facet of the industry.

- **Opportunities for Musicians**: Showcasing at SXSW can lead to booking deals, sync placements, and label interest. Many artists, including Billie Eilish and John Mayer, have gotten their big breaks at SXSW.

- **Why It's Key**: With so many key players in attendance, SXSW is a prime opportunity to network with professionals who can help you elevate your career. The sheer size and scope of the event make it an essential stop for anyone serious about building industry relationships.

2. ASCAP "I Create Music" Expo – Los Angeles, CA

What You Can Gain

The ASCAP "I Create Music" Expo is specifically designed for songwriters, composers, and producers looking to advance their careers. The event offers workshops on songwriting, publishing, and production, along with panels featuring top artists and industry executives. It's an excellent conference for those interested in expanding their songwriting network and gaining insider knowledge about the business side of music.

- **Opportunities for Musicians**: Attendees can participate in one-on-one feedback sessions with industry veterans, attend workshops, and learn about licensing, publishing, and royalties—critical knowledge for anyone in music.

- **Why It's Key**: The focused nature of ASCAP Expo makes it a valuable experience for those looking to strengthen their songwriting and business skills while networking with publishers, songwriters, and producers. It's also a fantastic opportunity to meet representatives from ASCAP, one of the largest performing rights organizations.

3. MIDEM – Cannes, France

What You Can Gain

MIDEM is a premier international music conference, where global professionals gather to discuss the latest trends in music tech, publishing, streaming, and rights management. While it's heavily industry-focused, MIDEM offers artists a chance to meet with labels, publishers, and tech companies to discuss collaborations, licensing, and distribution opportunities.

- **Opportunities for Musicians**: MIDEM is known for its emphasis on international music markets, making it an ideal conference if you're looking to expand your presence beyond your home country. You'll find opportunities to network with representatives from international record labels, publishers, and streaming platforms.

- **Why It's Key**: For artists looking to break into the global market, MIDEM offers unparalleled access to international professionals. The conference also hosts showcases, allowing selected artists to perform for a global audience of industry insiders.

4. Billboard Latin Music Week – Miami, FL

What You Can Gain

Billboard Latin Music Week focuses on Latin music's growing influence in the global market. It's a hub for Latin artists, producers, and industry professionals to connect and collaborate. With panels featuring top Latin artists, producers, and executives, this event is a must-attend for anyone involved in Latin music.

- **Opportunities for Musicians**: Billboard Latin Music Week is a great place to meet with labels, distributors, and marketing professionals focused on the Latin music market. If you're an artist or producer in the Latin genre, this is your chance to build relationships with key players.

- **Why It's Key**: Latin music has exploded globally, and this event is at the center of that growth. Attending gives you access to the people shaping the future of the genre and offers significant networking opportunities.

5. MUSEXPO – Los Angeles, CA

What You Can Gain

MUSEXPO is known for attracting top executives from the global music industry, including A&R reps, music supervisors, and digital media experts. The conference focuses on the future of the music business, discussing everything from sync licensing to streaming trends.

- **Opportunities for Musicians**: MUSEXPO offers a unique opportunity to meet sync licensing professionals, making it ideal for artists interested in getting their music placed in film, TV, and commercials. There are also networking sessions where artists can connect with international labels and publishers.

- **Why It's Key**: With a heavy emphasis on sync licensing and digital media, MUSEXPO is an essential conference for musicians looking to expand their reach through film, TV, and new media. The networking opportunities are invaluable for artists seeking to navigate the business side of music.

***Do You Know?** Do you know that attending music conferences like SyncSummit, MUSEXPO, and ASCAP "I Create Music" Expo can provide direct access to top music executives, sync supervisors, and industry insiders? These conferences are networking gold mines for serious artists looking to level up.*

6. SyncSummit – Multiple Locations

What You Can Gain

SyncSummit is specifically focused on sync licensing, bringing together artists, producers, and music supervisors who are looking to place music in film, TV, and advertising. This conference provides deep

insights into the sync process, including how to pitch your music, negotiate deals, and understand contracts.

- **Opportunities for Musicians**: At SyncSummit, you can connect directly with music supervisors and sync agents who are actively looking for music to place in visual media. The event also hosts workshops on how to tailor your music for sync placements.

- **Why It's Key**: If your goal is to get your music placed in film, TV, or commercials, SyncSummit is one of the best conferences to attend. The focused environment ensures that you're meeting professionals who are specifically in the sync industry, giving you a higher chance of landing deals.

7. AIMP Global Music Publishing Summit – New York, NY

What You Can Gain

The Association of Independent Music Publishers (AIMP) hosts this summit, focusing on the music publishing industry. It's an excellent event for artists, songwriters, and producers who want to learn more about publishing deals, royalties, and intellectual property rights.

- **Opportunities for Musicians**: If you're a songwriter or producer looking to understand the intricacies of publishing and royalties, this summit is packed with panels featuring top publishers and industry experts. You'll learn about the latest trends in music publishing, how to protect your work, and how to maximize your earnings.

- **Why It's Key**: Understanding publishing is critical to long-term success in the music industry. The AIMP Summit gives you access to publishing experts who can guide you on how to navigate the complex world of royalties and intellectual property, making it a must-attend for anyone looking to secure their financial future in music.

8. Canadian Music Week – Toronto, Canada

What You Can Gain

Canadian Music Week (CMW) is one of Canada's largest music industry events, bringing together professionals from around the world to discuss everything from artist management to music tech. The conference includes showcases, panels, and networking sessions with international industry representatives.

- **Opportunities for Musicians**: CMW provides performance opportunities for emerging artists, along with panels that discuss international touring, marketing strategies, and digital distribution. It's a great place to network with labels, managers, and booking agents.

- **Why It's Key**: If you're looking to expand your presence in North America or internationally, CMW offers access to industry professionals from multiple countries. The showcase opportunities can lead to booking gigs and expanding your fanbase across borders.

Why These Events Are Key to Building Industry Relationships

1. Direct Access to Decision-Makers

These conferences bring together the top decision-makers in the music industry—whether they are A&R reps, music supervisors, sync agents, or publishers. Attending these events allows you to pitch your music, build relationships, and create lasting connections that can lead to career-changing opportunities.

2. Networking with Peers and Future Collaborators

In addition to meeting industry professionals, these conferences provide an opportunity to connect with fellow musicians, producers, and songwriters. Many collaborations, tours, and even label signings have started with a conversation at a conference. Building relationships with your peers is just as important as connecting with executives, as they can become long-term collaborators and supporters.

3. Education and Industry Insights

Each conference offers panels and workshops led by industry experts, providing invaluable knowledge on how to navigate the music business. From learning about the latest trends in digital streaming to understanding the nuances of sync licensing, these events equip you with the tools you need to succeed in an ever-evolving industry.

4. Global Exposure and Expansion

Many of these conferences attract international professionals, making them ideal for expanding your music career globally. Whether it's connecting with international labels at MIDEM or learning about global sync opportunities at MUSEXPO, attending these conferences can help you break into new markets and build a worldwide audience.

Final Thoughts: Elevate Your Career Through Music Conferences

Attending music industry conferences is one of the best investments you can make in your career. These events provide access to the people and knowledge that can take your career to the next level. Whether you're looking for sync deals, label interest, or international exposure, the relationships you build and the insights you gain at these conferences will help you navigate the industry and unlock new opportunities.

6.2 How to Network Like a Pro at Conferences

Networking at music conferences is a game-changer for building professional connections that can push your career forward. But making those quick meet-and-greets turn into lasting, solid relationships takes some skill. It's not just about shaking a million hands—it's about creating real, genuine connections and knowing how to follow up the right way to keep the vibe strong after the event. In this section, we'll dive into strategies to help you get the most out of your networking opportunities and show you how to flip those initial interactions into long-term professional relationships.

Strategies for Turning Brief Interactions Into Lasting Professional Relationships

1. Set Clear Networking Goals Before the Conference

Before you even arrive at the conference, it's important to set clear networking goals. What do you want to achieve? Are you looking to meet sync supervisors, A&R reps, potential collaborators, or music tech entrepreneurs? Having a clear focus allows you to be more intentional with your time and interactions.

- **Research Key Attendees**: Many conferences provide lists of speakers, panelists, and attending companies ahead of time. Identify the people you want to connect with and research their background, recent projects, and interests. This will help you approach them with thoughtful questions or conversation starters, making your interaction more impactful.

- **Set Specific Goals**: Rather than aiming to meet as many people as possible, set specific goals such as "connect with three sync agents" or "meet at least two potential collaborators." This helps you stay focused and ensures that you're meeting people who align with your career objectives.

2. Perfect Your Elevator Pitch

A conference is a fast-paced environment, and you may only have a few minutes to introduce yourself to someone important. Having a well-prepared, concise elevator pitch is key to making a memorable impression. Your pitch should quickly communicate who you are, what you do, and what value you can bring to the person you're speaking to.

- **Be Brief and Engaging**: Your elevator pitch should be no longer than 30 seconds. Start with your name and your role in the industry (e.g., "Hi, I'm Sarah, a singer-songwriter specializing in indie folk."). Then, highlight your recent work or a unique selling point (e.g., "I just had a track placed in a major TV show."). End by expressing interest in their work or how you might collaborate in the future.

- **Tailor Your Pitch**: Adjust your pitch depending on who you're speaking with. If you're talking to a sync agent, focus on your recent placements or your experience with sync-friendly music. If you're speaking to a producer, emphasize your creative vision or what you're working on next.

3. Approach Networking with Authenticity and Curiosity

At conferences, people often get approached by many attendees looking for opportunities. To stand out, approach conversations with genuine curiosity rather than a transactional mindset. Instead of focusing on what the person can do for you, take an interest in their work, ask thoughtful questions, and find ways to connect on a personal level.

- **Start with a Compliment or Shared Experience**: Open the conversation by mentioning something specific you admire about the

person's work, such as a recent project they were involved in or a panel discussion they led. Alternatively, comment on a shared experience at the conference (e.g., "I really enjoyed that panel on sync licensing—your insights were spot on").

- **Ask Thoughtful Questions**: People appreciate when you show genuine interest in their work. Ask open-ended questions that allow them to talk about their experiences or upcoming projects. For example, "What's been the most exciting project you've worked on recently?" or "How do you see the industry evolving in the next few years?" This shows that you're engaged and opens the door for deeper conversations.

4. Be Strategic About Where You Network

Conferences can be overwhelming, and it's important to choose the right moments and locations to network. Large social events and mixers are great for casual conversations, while smaller panels or workshops might offer more focused opportunities to meet key players.

__Do You Know__? Do you know that following up after a conference is crucial? Studies show that 80% of professionals never follow up after initial networking meetings. Sending a personalized email or message within 24-48 hours keeps your new connection warm and increases your chances of forming long-term professional relationships.

- **Attend Networking Mixers and Social Events**: These events are specifically designed for networking, so people are expecting to meet new contacts. Approach conversations casually, but have your elevator pitch ready if the opportunity arises.

- **Focus on Smaller, Intimate Events**: Workshops, breakout sessions, or even coffee breaks often provide better opportunities for meaningful interactions because they're more intimate. In these smaller settings, you can engage in deeper conversations without the distractions of a large crowd.

- **Be Where Your Targets Are**: If you know certain industry professionals are speaking at or attending a panel, make sure to attend. It gives you a natural way to start a conversation afterward by referencing the discussion. For example, "I enjoyed your perspective on music publishing. I'd love to hear more about your thoughts on how artists can better protect their rights."

5. Have a Call to Action

After introducing yourself and having a conversation, it's important to end with a clear call to action that keeps the connection going beyond the conference.

- **Exchange Contact Information**: Ask for their business card or connect on LinkedIn during or right after the conversation. A simple "I'd love to stay in touch—can I grab your card?" ensures that you have a way to follow up later. If they're open to it, suggest connecting on social media platforms like Instagram or Twitter to stay engaged.

- **Suggest a Follow-Up**: If the conversation went well and there's a clear opportunity for collaboration or further discussion, suggest a specific follow-up, such as "I'd love to continue this conversation— maybe we could grab coffee next week?" or "I'll send over some of my tracks for you to check out."

Effective Follow-Up Techniques to Keep Your Connections Warm After the Event

1. Follow Up Within 24-48 Hours

Timing is crucial when following up after a conference. Aim to send a follow-up message within 24-48 hours while the interaction is still fresh in their mind. This shows that you're serious about maintaining the connection and helps you stand out from the crowd.

- **Personalize Your Follow-Up**: Avoid generic follow-up emails. Instead, reference something specific from your conversation to jog their memory. For example, "It was great meeting you at the Sync Licensing panel. I really enjoyed our conversation about how music supervisors are finding new talent through streaming platforms."

- **Be Brief but Clear**: Keep your message short and to the point. Reinforce your interest in staying connected and suggest next steps, such as setting up a meeting or sending over your work. For example, "I'd love to send you some of my recent tracks—let me know if you'd be interested!"

2. Connect on Social Media

Social media is a powerful tool for keeping your connections warm. After the conference, follow the people you've met on platforms like LinkedIn, Instagram, or Twitter. Engage with their posts by liking, commenting, or sharing their content when relevant. This helps you stay on their radar in a non-intrusive way and reinforces the relationship over time.

- **Send a Social Media Message**: If you connect on social media, follow up with a direct message thanking them for the conversation and expressing your interest in staying in touch. For example, "It was great meeting you at [conference]—I look forward to staying connected here."

- **Share Your Content**: If you have new music, articles, or projects that align with the person's interests, share them via social media. Just be sure not to overwhelm them with too much content at once.

3. Provide Value in Your Follow-Up

When following up, focus on how you can provide value to the person you've connected with. Whether it's offering to collaborate, sharing useful resources, or introducing them to someone in your network, providing value will help solidify the relationship.

- **Offer Something Helpful**: For example, if you discussed sync licensing, you might follow up by sharing a useful article or resource on that topic. Or if they're looking for a producer, you could offer to connect them with someone in your network who fits the bill.

- **Be Open to Collaboration**: If appropriate, suggest ways you could collaborate in the future. For example, "I'd love to collaborate on a project together—maybe we could explore some ideas for a future sync track?"

4. Maintain Consistent, Non-Intrusive Contact

Building long-term relationships requires consistent but respectful follow-up. After the initial follow-up, stay in touch periodically by checking in, sharing updates, or sending them relevant content. The key is to remain present without being pushy.

- **Check In Periodically**: Reach out every few months with a brief check-in. For example, "I wanted to touch base and see how things are going on your end—let me know if there are any opportunities for us to collaborate."

- **Update Them on Your Progress**: If you've made progress on a project or reached a career milestone, share it with your contact. For example, "I just had a track placed in a new Netflix series—would love for you to check it out!"

5. Attend Future Events

One of the best ways to keep your connections warm is by attending future industry events where they'll be present. This gives you the opportunity to reconnect in person and continue building the relationship.

- **Reconnect in Person**: If you know they're attending the same event, reach out beforehand to set up a time to meet or chat. For example, "I saw that you'll be at MIDEM this year—let's grab coffee and catch up!"

- **Maintain Visibility**: Regularly attending conferences and events where your contacts are present helps you maintain visibility within the industry and shows that you're committed to staying active in the music business.

Final Thoughts: Mastering the Art of Conference Networking

Networking at conferences is an invaluable opportunity to build meaningful, long-term relationships in the music industry. By setting clear goals, engaging authentically, and following up effectively, you can turn brief interactions into lasting professional connections. Remember that networking is not just about collecting business cards—it's about nurturing relationships that can lead to collaborations, sync deals, and career growth. With the right approach, you can leverage every conference to expand your network and take your music career to the next level.

6.3 Conference Success Stories

Attending music conferences can be a game-changer for artists, producers, and industry players. It only takes one solid connection or opportunity at a conference to flip the script—opening up new doors, giving your career that push, and putting you on game about the latest shifts in the industry. In this part, we're diving into real stories of people who hit up these events, made the right moves, and turned those networking moments into major steps forward. Eddie Caldwell's seen firsthand how these moments can spark a whole new chapter, and these stories show just how powerful those connections can be.

1. Billie Eilish – SXSW (South by Southwest)

Billie Eilish is a standout example of an artist who used SXSW as a platform to propel her career forward. In 2017, at just 15 years old, Billie performed at the influential Austin festival, showcasing her unique sound and presence. At the time, she was still relatively unknown, but her SXSW performance drew the attention of key industry professionals, further building on the momentum she had started with her viral track "Ocean Eyes."

- **The Impact**: Billie's SXSW performance helped solidify her reputation as a rising star, catching the attention of A&R reps and music supervisors. The exposure she gained from SXSW helped her connect with key figures who would later become instrumental in her success, including her future label, Interscope Records.

- **Key Takeaway**: Showcasing at industry-heavy conferences like SXSW can provide emerging artists with the exposure they need to attract key players in the music business. For Billie Eilish, SXSW was a springboard that helped accelerate her path to stardom.

2. Halsey – The New Music Seminar

Before becoming a global pop star, Halsey (then known as Ashley Frangipane) was navigating the music industry as an unsigned artist. One of her major breakthroughs came when she attended the New Music Seminar (NMS) in New York City, a conference known for giving emerging artists a platform to network with industry professionals. Halsey performed at the event, which helped her attract the attention of major label A&R reps.

> *"Success is not just about what you accomplish in your life, it's about what you inspire others to do."*

• **The Impact**: Halsey's performance at NMS, combined with her growing online following, led to meetings with several major record labels. Shortly after, she signed with Astralwerks, part of Capitol Records, which allowed her to release her debut EP *Room 93* and begin her rise to fame.

• **Key Takeaway**: For unsigned artists, conferences like the New Music Seminar offer a unique chance to showcase their talent in front of industry professionals. Halsey's ability to leverage her performance at NMS helped her land a record deal and kickstart her mainstream career.

3. Lizzo – ASCAP "I Create Music" Expo

Lizzo's rise to success was the result of years of hard work, networking, and building relationships in the music industry. Early in her career, she attended the ASCAP "I Create Music" Expo, a conference designed for songwriters, composers, and producers. At the expo, Lizzo networked with industry professionals, gaining insights into the songwriting and publishing world.

- **The Impact**: Through her connections at ASCAP Expo, Lizzo learned how to navigate the complex world of music publishing and royalties, setting her up for long-term financial success as her career took off. The knowledge and relationships she built at the conference were critical as she transitioned from an emerging artist to a chart-topping superstar.

- **Key Takeaway**: For artists like Lizzo, attending industry-specific conferences like ASCAP Expo can provide invaluable education and connections, especially in areas like publishing and royalties. These insights can be instrumental in building a sustainable career.

4. Chance the Rapper – A3C Festival

Before becoming an independent music icon, Chance the Rapper was making a name for himself in Chicago's local scene. A significant turning point in his career came when he attended and performed at the A3C Festival in Atlanta, one of the largest hip-hop conferences in the world. At A3C, Chance was able to network with other up-and-coming artists, producers, and industry professionals.

- **The Impact**: Chance's performance at A3C helped him gain national exposure and connect with influential figures in the hip-hop world. His networking efforts at the festival allowed him to build relationships that would later help him grow his independent music career, culminating in the release of his critically acclaimed mixtape *Acid Rap*.

- **Key Takeaway**: For independent artists like Chance the Rapper, attending genre-specific conferences like A3C provides opportunities to perform and network with key players in the industry. These connections helped Chance build a career on his own terms, outside of the traditional record label system.

5. John Legend – Sundance Film Festival

Before becoming a household name, John Legend attended the Sundance Film Festival, which, while primarily focused on film, is also known for its integration of music into the cinematic world. At Sundance, Legend performed at various events, where he connected with filmmakers, music supervisors, and industry professionals. This exposure helped him expand his reach beyond the music industry, leading to sync placements and collaborations in film and TV.

- **The Impact**: John Legend's networking efforts at Sundance helped him secure sync deals for his music in film and TV, broadening his audience and increasing his exposure. These placements played a role in building his brand as a versatile artist capable of crossing over into multiple entertainment sectors.

- **Key Takeaway**: Attending cross-industry events like Sundance can be a strategic move for musicians looking to expand their network beyond the music business. Sync placements and collaborations with filmmakers can open up new opportunities for exposure and revenue.

6. Kacey Musgraves – Americana Music Festival & Conference

Kacey Musgraves, known for blending country with pop and indie influences, found success by attending and performing at the Americana Music Festival & Conference. This event, focused on the Americana genre, allowed her to showcase her unique sound in front of music industry professionals who were open to non-traditional country music.

MUSIC OF THE SEA

- **The Impact**: Kacey's performance at the Americana Music Festival caught the attention of influential music writers and label representatives. This exposure helped her secure a record deal with Mercury Nashville, which eventually led to the release of her Grammy-winning album *Golden Hour*.

- **Key Takeaway**: For artists like Kacey Musgraves, genre-specific conferences and festivals can be crucial for getting noticed by industry insiders who are passionate about specific styles of music. Her performance at the Americana Music Festival helped her connect with the right people to support her career's growth.

7. Deadmau5 – Winter Music Conference

Electronic music producer Deadmau5's breakout moment came at the Winter Music Conference (WMC) in Miami, an event known for its focus on electronic dance music (EDM) and DJ culture. While attending the conference, Deadmau5 networked with influential DJs, producers, and promoters, which led to his music being played at major clubs and festivals around the world.

- **The Impact**: Through networking at WMC, Deadmau5 built relationships with key figures in the EDM scene, which helped him grow his career and become one of the most recognized names in electronic music. His collaborations with other artists and DJs at the conference were instrumental in expanding his reach.

- **Key Takeaway**: For producers and DJs, attending genre-specific events like the Winter Music Conference offers a chance to meet influential industry figures and collaborators. These connections can help an artist expand their network and get their music into the hands of the right people.

Final Thoughts: Conferences as Catalysts for Career Growth

The stories of artists like Billie Eilish, Chance the Rapper, and Halsey illustrate how attending music conferences can be a pivotal moment in an artist's career. These events provide opportunities to showcase your work, connect with industry professionals, and gain insights that can help you navigate the business side of music. Whether you're an emerging artist or an established professional, music conferences offer valuable platforms to level up your career through networking, education, and exposure. By strategically attending the right events and making the most of networking opportunities, you can open doors to new opportunities and take your career to new heights.

"The music supervisors at Creative Control are working on dozens of film, television, and games projects on any given day across a wide variety of genres and budgets. Eddie and Music Of The Sea is one of the very first calls we make when we are looking for Music. Because we know they will deliver in terms of quality and targeted creativity Every time"

Joel C High -

Music Supervisor
Tyler Perry Enterprises, Madea Franchise, Sovereign

Conclusion: Show Up and Show Out

As we've explored throughout *Volume 2: Show Up and Show Out*, building a successful career in the music industry requires more than just talent. It takes intentionality, persistence, and a deep understanding of how to navigate the ever-changing landscape of social media, live performances, collaborations, and professional networking. Whether you're an emerging artist looking to establish your brand or an experienced professional seeking to expand your reach, the strategies outlined in this book are designed to empower you to take control of your career and position yourself for long-term success.

> *"The best way to predict the future is to create it."*
>
> *– Peter Drucker*

1. Consistency is Key

From building your social media presence to engaging with fans and industry professionals, consistency is one of the most critical components of success. It's not enough to show up once—you have to keep showing up, providing your audience with content, performances, and engagement that keep you on their radar. Whether you're posting regularly on Instagram, engaging with followers, or creating scroll-stopping content, consistency will set you apart from the competition.

2. Collaborations Can Open Doors

One of the most effective ways to expand your audience and elevate your career is through collaboration. Whether it's working with other artists, producers, or even influencers, collaborations can bring fresh perspectives to your work, push your creative boundaries, and lead to new opportunities, including sync placements and brand partnerships. The music industry thrives on relationships, and collaborating with others can help you tap into new networks and reach broader audiences.

3. Networking and Building Industry Relationships

Music industry conferences, live showcases, and industry mixers are invaluable opportunities for making meaningful connections. Building professional relationships with executives, A&R reps, sync supervisors, and fellow artists is essential to growing your career. But it's not just about exchanging business cards—it's about nurturing those relationships, following up, and providing value. The strongest careers are built on the foundation of a solid network, and the more effort you put into building and maintaining those relationships, the greater your chances of long-term success.

4. Seize Every Opportunity

The industry is full of opportunities, but you have to be proactive in seeking them out. Whether it's volunteering at industry events, attending conferences, or being ready to perform at a moment's notice, positioning yourself in the right places at the right times is crucial. Opportunities won't always come knocking—sometimes you have to create them by showing up, staying ready, and taking risks.

5. Authenticity Wins

While it's important to adapt to the ever-evolving demands of the music industry, staying true to yourself and your artistic vision is what will ultimately make you stand out. Authenticity resonates with audiences and

industry professionals alike, and it's your unique voice and perspective that will attract lasting opportunities.

Whether you're performing live, engaging on social media, or collaborating with others, being genuine in your approach will build deeper connections with both fans and peers.

The Journey is Ongoing

The strategies, case studies, and insights shared in this book are not a one-size-fits-all formula, but rather a collection of tools and frameworks that you can adapt to your own journey. The music industry is constantly evolving, and so must you. Keep learning, keep networking, and keep pushing the boundaries of your creativity and professionalism.

Ultimately, *Show Up and Show Out* is a mindset. It's about being bold in your efforts, resilient in the face of challenges, and relentless in pursuing your goals. By showing up consistently, seizing every opportunity, and cultivating relationships, you can build a career that not only reflects your artistic vision but also creates lasting impact in the music world.

So, step out, show up, and show out—the stage is yours.

Contact Us

For inquiries, consultations, and submissions, please feel free to reach out via email:
Email: info@musicofthesea.com

For submissions, visit our submission page:
Submission Page: Music Licensing Submissions

Website: www.musicofthesea.com

Connect with us on social media:
Facebook: musicofthesea
Instagram: @musicofthesea
Twitter: @musicofthesea
Threads: @musicofthesea
TikTok: @musicoftheseasync

About the Author

Eddie Caldwell is the ultimate powerhouse behind Music Of The Sea Inc., a music empire with a jaw-dropping catalog of over 250,000 pre-cleared songs and cues from 2,000+ major and indie artists. Whether it's blockbuster hits or underground gems, Eddie's music has been the secret sauce behind some of the biggest moments in Hollywood and beyond.

You've heard his work in films like Guardians of the Galaxy Vol. 3, Once Upon a Time in Hollywood, The Shape of Water, and the Oscar-winning best picture CODA. His music isn't just in theaters—Eddie's magic has landed on your favorite shows, too, including Emmy Winners such as Ted Lasso, Better Call Saul, NCIS, Sex Education, and Hacks.

With an all-star roster featuring the likes of Snoop Dogg, Future, Marilyn Monroe, Billy Ray Cyrus, Lil Baby, Rick Ross, Ludacris, and more, Eddie has the golden touch when it comes to placing hits. Eddie has procured thousands and thousands of placements, from big-screen blockbusters to TV, video games, and even the restaurant you love—his music is everywhere, and you can feel it.

But Eddie doesn't just play the hits. He has deals with NBC/Universal, CBS/Paramount, Disney, Netflix, Omnicom, and others. He works closely with giants like Marvel and Warner Bros, securing music for the biggest shows and ads you know and love. He's even got a track from the

legendary Marilyn Monroe in his vault. Talk about iconic!
Through Music Of The Sea, Eddie has built a global music powerhouse, and this book gives you a front-row seat to how he did it—and how you can get in on the action. From the highs to the wild rides of the industry, Eddie's story is as electrifying as the music he represents.

Want to know the secrets behind music's biggest moments? Craving a peek into the world of A-list placements and international deals? Dive into Eddie Caldwell's world and discover how he turned his passion into a global sensation. This is more than just a story—it's an invitation to witness the magic of music like never before.

Ready to tune in? Grab your copy and get ready to ride the wave with Music Of The Sea!

www.ingramcontent.com/pod-product-compliance
Lightning Source LLC
Chambersburg PA
CBHW041958110726
48006CB00004B/928